A Handbook
for
Heretics

A Handbook
for
Heretics

A MODERN REFORMATION:

From Religion to
The Kingdom of God

By

John W. Sloat

Former Presbyterian Clergyman

ISBN 0-7414-1030-3

Published by:

PUBLISHING.COM

519 West Lancaster Avenue
Haverford, PA 19041-1413
Info@buybooksontheweb.com
www.buybooksontheweb.com
Toll-free (877) BUY BOOK
Local Phone (610) 520-2500
Fax (610) 519-0261

Printed in the United States of America

Printed on Recycled Paper

Published May, 2002

With Love And Appreciation To

The Bailey Group

The Greer Group

The Troxell Group

The Hubbard Group

The Oneness Fellowship

My Former Sunday School Class
At First Presbyterian Church

We invite you to visit our website
Beyond Religion
at
www.beyondreligion.com

and also
www.johnwsloat.com

TABLE OF CONTENTS

ACKNOWLEDGEMENTS

Writing a book is a long process which, in my case, could not have happened without the encouragement and input of many friends. It is not possible to recognize, or even remember, all those who helped in some way. But there are some whom I want to thank in print. I hope they know how grateful I am to all of them.

First, I want to thank God and my angels, chiefly Meredith, for the inspiration and insights I received while working on this manuscript. Their guidance throughout my life has helped prepare me for this work.

Second, I am grateful to my former presbytery for pressuring me to relinquish my pastoral ordination. Since there are no mistakes, this was part of the divine plan. Without their intervention I might never have written this book.

Third, I have a wonderful group of friends who have always supported and encouraged me. They have met with me in countless study group sessions to help refine this material. Their love and courage have been a major gift and I can never thank them enough. I need to name a few of them: Cindy, Laurie, Pat, Joyce, Karen, Kelly, Brigitte, Peg, Joe, Betty P., Mary Jayne, Joan, Norma, Eileen, Sandy, Dan, Jen, Cheryl, Mayada, Nina, Carol, Kim, David, Betty K. and John. Also, Susan, who returned to spirit during the development of this material, was of tremendous help, both before and after her departure. I feel that she was one of the guides who helped me edit the material. (She had been a high school English teacher!) I am also grateful to my former Sunday School class at The First Presbyterian Church in New Castle, PA which demonstrated that many people are eager to study this type of material. Also, my thanks goes to the two dozen people who read the manuscript and gave me valuable feedback.

Fourth, I want to thank Northminster Church, New Castle, PA, which I served as pastor for thirty-one years, for allowing me to stretch and grow during that time. The staff members with whom I worked there were especially helpful and supportive, and I will always cherish the time I spent with them. In addition, the church's dedication to its interfaith traditions, especially with the former Temple Israel in New Castle, added a new dimension to our search for a larger spiritual truth. Together, these two congregations created the Oneness Fellowship which attracted more than two hundred people over the years, proving that even in a traditionally conservative area there are many who are ready and anxious to enlarge their thinking.

Fifth, I am very grateful to Dr. Christopher M. Bache, a faculty member at Youngstown State University in Ohio and author of *Lifecycles: Reincarnation and the Web of Life*. Chris is a spiritual master who has been a mentor and inspiration to me over many years. Dr. David W. Cliness, a former faculty member at YSU, has also contributed great insight and energy to my personal investigations and deserves my profound thanks.

Finally, I thank my family. My wife, Helen, and our three children, Linda, Laurie and David, have supported, challenged and struggled with me through my long pilgrimage from orthodoxy to heresy. I am very grateful for their love, their belief in me, and the ways in which they have become my teachers.

J.W.S.

EXPLANATORY NOTE

Before we begin this consideration of the state of the Christian church at the beginning of the 21st century, it is necessary to make some distinctions.

The church is not a monolithic unity. It is an amalgam which runs the gamut from the highly ritualistic Orthodox traditions to the spontaneous experiences of Pentacostalism. In between are literally hundreds of variations, from liberal to conservative, from traditional to innovative, from other-worldly to socially-involved. Thus, no statement in a work of this kind can apply with equal relevance to all the various branches of the Christian institution.

My thoughts are aimed primarily at that section of the church referred to as mainline Protestantism, the area with which I am most familiar. Even within that narrow segment of the church there are broad variations. Some denominations and congregations have long since adopted the changes which I am suggesting here, and are pioneers who are spearheading the second reformation. Their existence provides a practical model for some of the ideas expressed in this book.

Nevertheless, I am addressing the broad range of traditional Protestant and Reformed churches—and to some extent the Roman Catholic and Eastern Orthodox traditions—which are still locked in the forms and the theology developed over the past two millennia. Great portions of the church seem to be unaware of the distinction between institutional tradition and personal spirituality, between demanding to be in control and allowing God to be in control. It is this portion of the church about which I am most concerned and to whom my remarks are most pointedly directed. The reader can decide if and where these comments apply.

When I use the term "the church," it can be read as "The Christian Church." However, I am making a distinction between the Christian church and the Christian faith. The faith is a body of spiritual beliefs; the church consists of the traditions and institutions through which those beliefs are interpreted and expressed in daily practice.

J.W.S.

PREFACE

We are in the middle of a second reformation. The reformation of the 1600s came about as a result of the church's involvement in secular politics. Distracted by wealth and power, it had abandoned its original purpose, to be a spiritual force in the physical world, to help establish the Kingdom of God on earth. Those who broke from the established church wanted to restore its spiritual dimension and reclaim the right to think for themselves. As a result, they were labeled heretics.

The current reformation is also the result of the church's involvement in politics. But this time it is religious politics. Much of the church is so busy defending its tradition and protecting its power that it has once again turned its back on its spiritual commission. It has confused winning members for the institution with winning souls for the Kingdom. The fact that the church cannot see the distinction between these two realities, the institution and the Kingdom, is at the heart of the problem. Many current and former members want to be free to think for themselves, to discover what spiritual truths may lie outside the bounds of the church's tradition. But those who try to do so are still labeled heretics.

The tension within the church is caused by two different schools of thought.

• One is comprised of those who believe that revelation is an ongoing process, that God is immanent and intimately involved in the daily life of humankind. These people believe Jesus literally when he says, "I have much more to tell you,"[1] and "I am with you always."[2] With those two promises, Jesus indicates that being his disciple involves remaining open to the guidance and inspiration of the Holy Spirit.

• The other includes people who believe that the revelation is complete, that God has spoken the final word, and that discipleship means adhering to the tradition and the confessions of faith. But believing that the truth has been fully revealed means defending that truth against change, and this results in the conviction that any further so-called "revelation" is either misguided or demonic.

This modern reformation comes out of a period of explosive spiritual discovery in which God is showering us with fresh data about the reality, structure and nearness of the spiritual world. Several years ago, a friend and I launched a website dealing with some of these current spiritual phenomena. We hoped to provide a bridge between the two schools of thought, the traditionalists and the millions of people who have had non-traditional spiritual experiences.

But much of this new information is rejected by the church because it conflicts with its time-honored theology. This rejection was demonstrated when my denomination took one look at our website, labeled it heresy, and forced me out of the ministry in which I had served for forty-three years.

The church needs to confront the reasons why it is losing members, why so many people find it less and less relevant, and why there is such a wealth of extraordinary spiritual experiences being reported by ordinary people. These people, far from being heretics, have discovered that Jesus meant it literally when he said that he had much more to tell us. They are the ones for whom this book is written. I want to let them know they are not alone, to offer support for their point of view, and to provide material which they can use in study groups.

The following chapters describe the new reformation which is taking place in our day and show that those whom the church often labels as heretics are actually the leading edge of a new spiritual age. The church must decide whether it will continue to focus on the past, ignoring what God is doing today, or whether it will open itself to the continuing revelation and become part of this new dispensation.

J.W.S.
January, 2002

THE THESIS OF THIS BOOK

We are embodied spirits.
We have both a physical and a spiritual dimension.

Therefore, we approach God in two different ways.
The physical way is called religion.
The non-physical way is called spirituality.

The difference between religion and spirituality
is the difference between Christianity and the Kingdom of God.

The church speaks for Christianity.
The Holy Spirit speaks for the Kingdom of God.

Christianity is a school of faith which helps us learn the basics of
morality and religious tradition. This is a collective experience.
The career for which that school of faith prepares us is life in the
Kingdom of God. This is an individual experience.

Those who interpret the Christian story literally, using their physical
senses, are called orthodox by the church.
Those who interpret the Christian story metaphorically, using their
spiritual senses, are called heretics by the church.

All of us have both literal and metaphorical elements in our
understanding of divine truth.
Therefore both groups, the orthodox and the heretical, are called to
live together in the church in peace.

To do so is to be obedient to Jesus who said:
"There are other sheep which belong to me that are not in this sheep
pen. I must bring them, too; they will listen to my voice, and they will
become one flock with one shepherd." John 10:16 TEV

I

NEWTON'S FIRST LAW

Sir Isaac Newton stated, in his first law of motion, that:

"An object...in motion tends to stay in motion with the same speed and in the same direction unless acted upon by an unbalanced force."

This law is not limited to objects. It is equally true of institutions. For instance, if a religion is going in a specific direction, it will continue on in that same direction. Forever.

Unless acted on by an "unbalanced" force.

Chapter 1

PROGRESS BEGINS WITH HERESY

I am a heretic.

I know this is true because my former presbytery branded me a heretic. I might as well admit that right up front.

Several hundred years ago they might have burned me at the stake. But because it was the year 2000, they merely burned me in effigy by revoking my ordination as a Presbyterian minister. It's surprising how little has changed since the 15th century. The Inquisition mentality still dominates large parts of the church.

People have asked me how it feels to be a heretic.

"Doesn't it bother you to be kicked out of the ministry after 43 years?"

"What makes you think you know more than all the authorities in the church?"

"Aren't you afraid of God's punishment?"

"Isn't it lonesome being outside the church?"

Actually, I'm in good company. St. Paul was a heretic. Galileo was a heretic. Calvin and Luther were heretics. Darwin was a heretic. Billy Mitchell was a heretic. The brew of history bubbles with heresy. Any break with tradition is labeled heretical at the start. And, of course, the greatest heretic of all was Jesus of Nazareth. That's why they killed him.

Jesus told us we would do greater things than he did.[3] I once thought this meant that we would perform greater miracles than he had. But perhaps he meant that we should become even greater heretics than he was. Think about it.

How can we claim to be disciples of this Galilean change-agent if we are opposed to change?

He was put to death by religious officials who were trying to protect their own power.[4] How can we be his followers if we are afraid to confront the entrenched religious power of our day?

He said that the Holy Spirit would lead us into *all* the truth.[5] How can we take that promise seriously and still allow church tradition to come between us and the Spirit's revelations?

I believe that Jesus calls us to creative heresy. His life was a sustained effort to crack through the hard outer shell of religious tradition in order to get down to the soft inner meat of spirituality. And he calls us to join him in that struggle. He says repeatedly, "Follow me." But he couples that challenge with a warning that discipleship has painful consequences: "If anyone wants to come with me, he must forget himself, *carry his cross,* and follow me."[6] He told us that his revelation about God was not complete, that he had much more to tell us.[7] He knew that if we took this promise seriously we would always be at odds with those who wanted to establish the institution, close the canon, and adopt the conclusive statement of faith.

Staying within the orthodox tradition usually keeps people out of trouble because they accept the approved standards of the *past*. But sincerely following Christ can get us into trouble because he holds before us a vision of the *future*. In this way, he calls us not to be followers but leaders, people who understand that today is a day of revelation, people whose desire is to raise the consciousness of the world. And when we choose that path, we encounter a predictable sequence in our spiritual growth:

As we open up spiritually, we begin to understand things which we were not ready to see previously.

As we understand more about God, we lose the fear which motivates so much of religion.

As we lose our fear, we dare to search beyond the limits which others have set for us.

But when we try to stretch the boundaries of orthodoxy, we come into conflict with authority.

Therefore, we are faced with an inescapable conclusion: to truly long for God, for a larger truth, is to risk being labeled "heretic." The establishment constantly seeks to ferret out and neutralize those who disagree with it. Why? Because heretics demand change. And orthodoxy cannot tolerate change.

History abounds with stories of dreamers who ran up against an unyielding establishment anxious to protect its own power. St. Paul is a classic example. The two sides of his nature—the orthodox and the visionary—were so distinct that they had different names. Saul was the name given to his physical, Jewish, pharisaical, establishment persona. He retained some of the characteristics of that side of his personality all through his life. But the discovery of his spiritual side, his connectedness to God, was so radically life-altering that he had to find a different name for the new person it produced; that name was Paul.

Becoming aware that he had two sides, however, immediately threw Paul into crisis because those sides were diametrically opposed. His horizontal self kept him in touch with his culture, his history, his daily human experience. During his earlier life, when he had been aware only of his orthodox self, he could live an untroubled existence, obeying the Law, pursuing those who did not agree with him, smug in the knowledge of his own religious superiority. But the discovery of his vertical dimension destroyed his complacent little world. Suddenly he was dazzled by the light, touched by God, able to hear the risen Christ speak to him, capable of seeing the highest heaven, ready to receive his commission to evangelize the world. His conversion shattered his earlier convictions and made him realize that there had to be major changes in his worldview. And that, of course, made him a threat to those who thought it was their duty to defend the tradition.

Paul realized that both dimensions were essential if he was to complete his mission. He said, "I become all things to all men, that I may save some of them by whatever means are possible."[8] He meant that he had to be able to function on both planes if he was going to be of use in helping establish the Kingdom of God on earth. His spiritual vision had to be expressed in his daily life, and his physical labors had to be directed by the Spirit. And these two dimensions came together in Saul/Paul to form a cross, a crisis. He could not escape into either one for safety. But trying to hold them both in tension marked him as a heretic.

That crisis happens, to some extent, in the life of anyone who allows a larger vision to invade his life. The Spirit makes obvious the need for change, but change always threatens those who are determined to hold on to their power in the old order. This conflict happens in all areas of life, not just in religion.

It happened to Galileo. In his case, the church was so dominant that even in matters of science it could charge heresy. His vertical, non-establishment perception of reality came from a desire for knowledge. The church, more interested in stability than knowledge, had always viewed the universe as perfect and unchangeable. It feared that, if someone demonstrated that the world was capable of change, all sorts of other things might also change, including the power structure of the church. So its position was based not on a desire for truth but on political necessity. For them, ironically, the truth was heretical. Truth is often opposed by politics. But in the battle between truth and entrenched power, truth eventually wins. Even the church could not ultimately keep Galileo's ideas from universal acceptance.

The same thing happened to Darwin. His research revealed that then-current theories about biological history were inadequate. But his vision of a larger truth, detailed in *The Origin of Species*, contradicted the creation narratives in Genesis. The religious establishment insisted that ancient truth was the last word and that any attempt to argue with scripture was blasphemy. The Scopes "Monkey Trial" was a classic example of categorical thinking blindly defending itself against the facts. Thinkers always prevail over closed minds because truth is on their side.

The case of General Billy Mitchell is an example of the same thing in a different arena. His court martial was a military version of a heresy trial. He had a clear vision of the potential of air power, and made a prediction as early as 1925 that the Japanese would launch a sneak attack against Pearl Harbor. But his ideas were opposed by admirals who had a vested interest in maintaining the supremacy of their naval forces. Time eventually produced the changes Mitchell demanded, but not before his career was ruined. His judges included no one connected with military aviation and their verdict was overturned by history.

The message is clear. Innovation often receives its impetus from heresy. Joseph Heller once said, "All good work is done in defiance of authority." But in religious circles that innovation is impeded by "the seven last words of the church" —*We've Never Done It That Way Before.* If the establishment believes it has the final truth, then any new idea will seem unorthodox. And yet, as demonstrated by these historical cases and thousands of others, it is the heretic and not the defender of orthodoxy who is often seen as the hero at the end of the day. The irony is that those who claim to be committed to the truth frequently are guilty of trying to prevent the truth from coming to light.

The church desperately needs *creative* heretics. A "creative heretic," an independent thinker, is an example of the "unbalanced" force to which Newton refers in his first law of motion. Only the person who breaks with tradition can change the direction of an institution. A heretic, as we have demonstrated, is not necessarily an enemy of God but may be one who is more interested in truth than in tradition. It takes courageous spiritual leadership to risk the hostility of those who fear change. But that courage will be rewarded if the church can be saved from death by irrelevance.

I love the church even though it has marginalized me. I am not speaking about the whole church because there are many places where it is alive, open, and growing. But there are many more places where it has become calcified and colorless, endlessly repeating ancient formulas which no longer inspire its own people, to say nothing of the unchurched public. Too many congregations have lost the tension between vision and practicality which can turn them into spiritual powerhouses. Many longtime church members are desperately seeking for something more, for a family of faith in which God is an exciting daily presence and where today's spiritual renaissance is recognized and honored.

We are in the midst of a second reformation. This is not to overstate the case. As the 16th century reformers had the courage to accept the label of heretic, so we must choose the side on which we will stand in this current religious paradigm shift. Traditionalists are essential, but they cannot save a church too often mired in meaningless routine. The only ones who can do that are those who have seen a vision of a living connection to God beyond religion. It is time for them to identify themselves and take up the cross of heresy. When enough of us are ready to risk our peaceful existence as well as our reputations, the church will discover the energy and the leadership it needs to recreate itself.

II

THE YELLOW DOOR

One fall day, my study was transformed by a mystical vision. It only happened once during the thirty-one years I worked in that room.

The study contains four doors: the entrance, two closets and a lavatory. All four doors are painted white. On this particular day, I came back after the morning service to hang up my robe. But as I went to open the closet door, I stopped in astonishment. The door was alive with glowing, golden light. While the other three doors looked normal, flat white, this one was radiant, brilliant. At first I wondered what was happening? An angel appearance? A burning bush in two dimensions?

I turned and looked out the window. Across the parking lot stood an immense oak tree perhaps sixty feet in height. It was October in Pennsylvania and the tree was an enormous ball of yellow leaves, blazing under the noonday sun. The angle was such that the reflected light shone directly onto my closet door.

I was so struck by the effect that I sat down at my desk and stared at the door. It not only glowed, it seemed to move. There was a vitality in the light that animated my door. I was fascinated by the display of an infinite variety of golden shades dancing together.

Then the image gradually began to fade. The gold turned to white again, leaving the painted wood flat and lifeless. I ran outside and looked at the sky. A large cloud covered the sun but the sky was mostly clear. Hurrying back to my chair, I sat staring at the door in anticipation.

Suddenly, the flat white surface got lighter, warmer, then blazed into life again. It was a stupendous effect. The sun and the tree were combining to create this display, just for me. Brilliant, dancing, exquisite yellow light.

I wondered to myself: What if I had never seen a tree before? Suppose this reflection on my door was the only evidence I had to tell me what a "tree" is? And how could I ever learn of the sun merely from watching these moving images? Immediately, Plato's cave came to mind, the classical illustration of a man chained in a cave, facing the back wall, trying to deduce from the shadows he saw there what was happening behind him outside the cave. Now God had given me my own private cave.

I turned to look at the tree again. From where I sat, it was close enough that I could see much of its detail. The high points of light on the outer leaves created pockets of mottled shadow further inside the tree where darker details of the tree's structure could be seen. Sprinkled through the golden covering were scarlet dots, leaves of a darker color, heightening the warmth of the overall effect. As a breeze blew through the tree, the leaves turned over showing their whitish backsides and sending ripples of lighter color spilling through the yellow mass. The tree was alive, crammed with detail, intricate far beyond my ability to take it all in.

I looked back at the door. The images were still moving and glowing, but all the detail was missing. Somehow, after seeing the real tree, the door was disappointing. It gave lovely hints of what a tree might be but, as beautiful as it was, the door would never tell me that the real tree was infinitely more beautiful.

Chapter 2

A SECOND REFORMATION

I am a Christian.

I am not the kind of Christian who is acceptable to my former presbytery, but it is not their approval I seek. My goal is spiritual. I am seeking oneness with God and with all of God's creation. I hope I am the kind of Christian who will emerge as a result of the second reformation. The "new" Christians will understand and follow Jesus on an entirely different level of awareness. This new awareness is at odds with a church which has, in too many areas, ceased to imitate Jesus because it is driven primarily by fear, outworn tradition and institutional politics. Jesus said he goes before us.[9] The church insists on looking backward for its authority. This is a fatal disconnection.

The title of this book implies that the modern reformation will be inspired by so-called Christian "heretics." The previous chapter detailed this process, describing how heresy can be a tool to stimulate change. In this chapter we will examine the need for a second reformation.

The church will no doubt continue in its present form in many quarters after the birth of the new Christianity, as the Jewish faith survived the Christian defection and the Roman Catholic church continued to exist after the original Reformation. But I believe that a large number of current and former church members, as well as many who have never been interested in the church as it is currently constituted, are ready for a major change, the birth of a new and more vital Christian faith.

As I said, I am a Christian. I was baptized at three months, confirmed at age twelve and ordained to the gospel ministry a dozen years later. I have been pastor/head of staff in two churches, one of which I served for thirty-one years, then was interim pastor in two other churches and finally spent three years as a visitation minister. In retirement I continue to worship in a local church where I am active in the ministry of music. I say all this merely to list my credentials and to

11

indicate that I love the church and have dedicated my life to serving God through it.

Therefore, I desire to see the church thrive and recapture its divine mission. But the church today is in trouble. No less an authority than Thomas W. Gillespie, president of Princeton Theological Seminary, the premier pastoral training center for the Presbyterian Church, recently referred to his denomination as "sick and dying."[10] Bishop John Spong speaks of the fact that our religious culture is characterized everywhere by spiritual people and dying churches. We have a shortage of pastors and priests because life in the parish is bureaucratic and demanding and leaves little time for spiritual growth. The Roman Catholic church is opposed to marriage for priests; Protestant churches in many cases fail to see women and gays and minorities as equal partners in ministry. We don't seem to be getting the message: We are living in a time of robust interest in spiritual truth, but much of that energy is being rejected by a church which is imprisoned in its own past.

The church has been losing members, support and influence for decades because, by focusing on the past and ignoring the revelations of the present, it is becoming increasingly irrelevant. People point to the resurgence of evangelical faith as evidence that the church is still healthy, but this is actually a negative indicator. In the same way that a patient rallies before death or a light bulb glows brightest just before it burns out, this activity signals a desperate effort to hold off the inevitable paradigm shift. Unfortunately, this rear-guard action is doomed to failure. We cannot solve this problem by simply doing more of what we've always done.

I stated that my personal goal is oneness with God and with all of God's creation. By contrast, the goals of traditional Christianity are often political. The church is not interested in oneness with all of God's creation because the heart of its message is divisiveness. It seeks to separate people into groups which it can then label as acceptable or unacceptable—Christian or non-Christian, Protestant or Catholic, orthodox or heretical, saved or unsaved, blessed or damned, straight or gay, male or female, conservative or liberal. It does this in a sincere effort to preserve its orthodoxy. But orthodoxy is not truth. It is merely our current understanding of truth. As long as Christianity claims to be the only door to the Kingdom of God, it will continue to reject those who believe that the Kingdom is a spiritual reality which unites all people regardless of religious tradition.

Since the church believes it has the final truth, it thinks it can speak for God. And thus it stops listening to God and listens only to its own message. There is a word for this behavior: idolatry. In its present form, the church is frequently doing exactly the opposite of its stated mission. This is because, instead of being open to the Spirit, it teaches exclusively from documents which are two millennia old. There is a subtle subterfuge at work here. The church refuses to listen to any current word from the Lord, and so it never hears anything new. This is because it remains trapped inside its own circular reasoning: The Bible tells the church what to believe, and the church declares the Bible to be the only rule for faith and practice. Until it breaks out of that cycle, it will remain deaf to the voice of God.

When the church focuses exclusively on the past, it makes a startling confession: it is afraid of God. It fears that if it expands its theology to embrace newer visions of God, it will lose its identity and its authority, be forced to give up control of its religious game and have to start all over again. So to protect its smaller truth, it sacrifices a larger truth. It acts out its belief that tradition is more important than revelation. When the church is afraid of God, something is terribly wrong!

Someone has written that the difference between adults and children is that adults don't ask questions. They think they already know all the answers. The church is much more interested in giving old answers than in asking new questions. This is why Jesus told us that it will be children and not "grown-ups" who see the Kingdom. When the church begins asking fresh questions, it will discover a whole new future for itself.

We need a second reformation. We are still plagued by the same kind of errors which necessitated the first. This time the remedies need to be on a far larger scale. For instance:

- Roman Catholicism claimed to be the one true church. Some still hold this opinion, although a majority recognize that there are other legitimate branches of the Christian church. Today we see the concept of "one true church" as short-sighted and chauvinistic. Yet a majority of Christians still believe that theirs is the one true religion.

- The reformation rejected the pope, disavowing the idea that a single individual's interpretations could be binding on all of Christendom. Yet, the church has elevated its confessions of faith to the same position so that these historic documents dictate the faith and practice of millions of believers. If a belief is not in the ancient standards, we are taught, it cannot be an acceptable part of the church's theological worldview. And so the church closes its ears to what God is saying today.

- One of the major ideas to emerge from the reformation was "the priesthood of all believers," the notion that all believers have equal access to God and that no one needs a priest to intercede for him. The church still lifts up this concept in theory although it appears to distrust it in practice. The spiritual experiences of lay people are often written off as imagination or ignorance while the "professionals" become the final authority in matters of theology. The clergy tends to be less open to new spiritual insights than the laity because of a natural tendency to defend their authority and careers against the threat posed by change.

13

- Luther's great theme was "salvation by faith alone." He believed that a sincere personal faith in Christ is what brings salvation, not works righteousness and religious practice. Protestants still hold this as an essential article of faith, but see it as true exclusively within the context of the church. If we actually believed in salvation by faith alone, we would understand that salvation is a spiritual reality and perfectly possible outside of organized religion.

- Indulgences were one of the primary issues addressed by Luther. An indulgence was a payment to the church which was thought to guarantee the donor's escape from the punishment of purgatory. For perhaps a majority of people today, church membership is an indulgence which insures against hell and promises heaven. The church does little to discourage this point of view. Until faith is seen as a free and joyous union with God, we will have missed the essential nature of the divine relationship. The church still uses fear to frighten people into obedience.

- The reformers denied the infallibility of church councils, saying that the church's leadership can and has erred. This is an admission that the church can never be perfect and must constantly be brought into line with the will of God. One of the standard themes of the church in which I was trained is "reformed and ever reforming." But in too many cases, any attempt at change is seen as an assault on the truth of God. How can a church which refuses to reform itself ask its people to change their ways?

- Luther recognized varying degrees of inspiration among those who wrote scripture. For instance, he had no love for the Letter from James or for The Revelation. The Bible contains practices which we consider abhorrent today: bigamy, child killing, slavery, summary execution. Yet the church, which sees scripture as its only authority, tends to view all of it as equally inspired. At the same time, it rejects the massive spiritual literature currently being published, some of which, I am quite certain, will be recognized one day as modern scripture.

We agree that an institution such as the church must define itself or lose its organizational identity. It has a perfect right to say, "Do this, believe that, and you will belong to our fellowship. If you refuse to concur, we will still love you but we will not consider you one of us." A worldwide institution like the church, in its effort to remain true to its principles, must of necessity be cautious about change. But the church today seems to be resisting any kind of change.

We must wonder why those who loudly proclaim their devotion to God are so afraid of actually letting God guide them. Their focus on tradition rather than inspiration reveals that the issue is actually a struggle for control. When "truth" is contained in a neat theological formula, all we have to do is memorize and enforce it. But when we open ourselves to God's inspiration, we can no longer anticipate what will happen. The rules become confused, we are uncertain what to believe and what to ignore, *and we run the risk of being wrong.* So we often settle for tradition because it is much less disturbing and more easily managed.

How do we find the courage, not to forsake our tradition, but to step back from it and ask, "Is there any word from the Lord?"

The church is like my old study, a small box with one window on the world. As the light of the Kingdom comes through our window and displays itself on our theological wall, it is vague and out of focus. We are forced to make guesses about what it means. Thus, elements which we understand, like fear and division and mistrust and punishment and imperfection, creep into our interpretation. We have come up with a very creative story about the Kingdom, but we are unaware that our perception of the "tree" only looks vaguely like the original.

Our box cannot contain the reality of the tree. We have tried for two millennia to cram the Kingdom into our limited ecclesiastical space, but in so doing we have had to cut off many of its branches to make it fit. Thus we are left with a distorted idea of what the tree actually looks like because we continue to examine only the bits and pieces we have dragged into our room. We need to look out the window if we are ever to see the actual tree.

But…we are afraid to do so. If we glance out the window, we may be forever discontented with the beautiful image on our wall. So we are stuck with a dilemma: settle for the fuzzy but familiar picture, or face the light and take our chances. I believe—and this is key—that we do not have to leave our room to face in a new direction. Looking out the window rather than worshipping the shimmering image on the wall is the simple move which will allow us to join the modern reformation. We can do so as Christians, but it will be a new kind of Christianity with a much more accurate picture of what the Kingdom tree actually looks like.

III

COLUMBUS

Christopher Columbus was a brave man. He had the courage to act upon his beliefs even though those beliefs had not been proven and ran contrary to popular opinion. He was convinced that the world was a sphere. Some who sailed with him were just as certain that the world was flat and that they were in danger of sailing off the edge into oblivion.

But while Columbus had a vision, there was much that he did not know. For one thing, he thought the world was a lot smaller than it is. His vision could not conceive of an entire continent as yet undiscovered by Europeans. That gap in his knowledge shrank the earth, made him think that it consisted only of those lands with which he was already familiar. Thus, he assumed, if he sailed far enough west he would bump into the east end of the continent upon which he was standing.

He risked his life on that theory, chasing the setting sun in the certainty that he was heading toward India. And events appeared to prove him correct. Thus, it was logical to call the native people whom he encountered "Indians."

Looking for the old world, he discovered an entire new world. But his preconceived notions kept him from recognizing the truth. He found what he expected to find, not what was really there.

Chapter 3

THE LOSS OF INNOCENCE

Heretics are created by God.

That sounds like a self-serving statement, coming from someone who has been labeled a heretic. But God seems to call innovators into service when institutions stop listening to the Holy Spirit. Apparently that's the only way God can get the momentum started again.

In the first two chapters, we stated that we need a modern reformation and that heretics will lead the charge. Now let's consider what makes a heretic. Where do they come from?

History has shown us that life seems to generate the independent thinkers it requires in order to push itself forward. And they often appear at just the right time with just the right skills to initiate the specific changes which need to be made. But, since the word "heretic" is almost always used in its pejorative sense, many people assume that heresy is an evil thing and they wonder who would want to become one. That reminds me of a line from *Annie* when Miss Hannigan says to herself, "Why any kid would want to be an orphan is beyond me." No one sets out to become an orphan or a heretic. It just happens.

Heretics, creative thinkers, innovators, seem to appear just when we need them, despite the high cost of living in opposition. They do so because they can't help themselves. Having seen a brighter light ahead of them, they are not willing to walk back into the shadows. Some inner force compels them forward with a power greater than their fear of the hostility which awaits them. That force is God. Since God knows that change is necessary for the continuation of life, God provides a steady supply of change agents by selecting individuals to lead the way. How this happens is a mystery, but apparently it is part of the divine plan. And those who are called to serve in this way usually wonder why they should have been singled out for such a questionable honor.

The tension between the two camps is caused by a fundamental difference in the way we view things. Traditionalists see change as a negative disregard for the obvious truth. Innovators view change as a positive commitment to a higher truth. The disagreement is complicated by the fact that both sides contain elements of the truth. It matters little who wins the argument, however, because where truth is concerned the majority is not always right.

Our best efforts to understand the truth are part fact, part distortion, part ignorance. The majority opposed Paul and Galileo and Billy Mitchell. Members of the majority, to prove that the heretics were wrong, wrote learned treatises about who God is and how the world operates and which weapons system is best. But those opinions had no more effect on reality than does a child's faith in Santa Claus. The truth eventually makes itself known despite how we may misunderstand it in the process. We are still evolving intellectually and spiritually, and those who emerge as "heretics" may simply understand this more clearly than others.

The first flickering of heresy occurs when a person examines a belief that has always been taken for granted and suddenly discovers that it no longer makes sense.

A certain little boy enjoyed the ritual of putting cookies and milk out for Santa on Christmas eve. He came downstairs one Christmas morning, when he was a little older, looked at the half-eaten cookie on the plate and was struck by a shocking thought. How did he know that those teeth marks had actually been made by Santa? There could be another explanation. His deductive powers told him to reconsider what he had always been taught.

This was an "aha" moment when the light suddenly broke through. But we often try to defend ourselves against that light. Like Columbus, we reinforce our assumptions by not questioning them, even when the evidence stares us in the face. We force people to be "Indians" when they are something altogether different, simply because that label fits our limited worldview. We force God to be something smaller than the truth because our perceptions cannot contain a larger reality. In the same way that a child eventually learns the true identity of the Easter Bunny and the Tooth Fairy, we have to be willing to give up our childish preconceptions. To do so always involves a loss of innocence; it is called growing up.

Many believers have had this kind of revelation. They discover that ideas which they had always accepted without question do not hold up on closer examination. That realization may make them feel guilty or cause them to fear that they are losing their faith. (It's important to point out here that doubt is not the opposite of faith. If faith is living in the presence of God, then sin is its opposite, living with indifference toward God. Doubt is an essential part of faith. Without the ability to doubt, which is part of God's gift of rational thinking, we would never be able to develop a mature faith.)

THE LOSS OF INNOCENCE

How many basic doctrines can a person question and still call himself a Christian? When do we cross the line between merely being a doubter and being a full-blown heretic? Some sects make it a sin to question *any* aspect of the faith. Thus, many people never give themselves permission to reexamine basic doctrines for themselves.

How many of us have ever looked objectively at what we were taught in Sunday School? A large percentage of church members still hold a junior high view of the faith, since that was the last time they attended classes. When we look critically at our belief system for the first time, it can be a shock. It can make us wonder why we never saw the inherent flaws in some of our traditional beliefs. Let's look at a few of these basic assumptions.

God has had nothing to say in the past 2000 years.

The biblical canon contains nothing written after the middle of the second century because no further documents were judged to be of scriptural quality. The motive behind this action was control. Closing the canon allowed the church to claim that the revelation was complete which in turn made possible the development of a fixed theological system which could be enforced.

This was a mistake. Scripture comes to us through the inspiration of the Holy Spirit. If the Spirit could reveal God's truth in the first century, it can reveal that truth just as easily in the twenty-first. In fact, Jesus promised that he had much more to tell us and that we would receive this information through the Holy Spirit.[11]

The original books of the Bible were not seen as "holy" when they first appeared. They were attempts to record how people witnessed the activity of God in their lives and in the life of their nation. That process continues today. New witnesses, inspired by the Holy Spirit just as surely as were the authors of the sixty-six books of the Bible, are sharing their understanding of God's activity in today's world. Some of these writings contain God's word to us just as clearly as the scriptural documents. To ignore these current revelations because of our fixation on a collection of ancient documents is to risk turning devotion into idolatry.

Jesus himself assures us that he will be a constant presence in our lives. In addition to his promise that he has much more to tell us, he also says, "I will be with you always,"[12] and "Where two or three are gathered in my name, there am I in the midst of them."[13] What is the purpose of his being with us except to instruct and guide us? When we fail to honor this current revelation, we create a problem. We are forced to stuff every present-day situation into thought patterns which are long out of date. Thus, we come to distorted conclusions, such as the belief that women are second class beings unworthy of ordination. Limiting ourselves to the Bible gives us permission to endlessly rehash ideas which are so familiar that they have lost much of their meaning. It also teaches us to shut our minds against what God is saying in our time.

We came from nowhere but will live for eternity.

Christians believe that when they die they will go to heaven where they will live in glory for eternity. They also believe that their life began at the moment they were conceived in their mother's womb. But this idea confuses time with eternity.

If a thing has a beginning, it will have an end. If a thing has no end, it could not have had a beginning. There is no way to avoid this reality, even in theology. My body may have been created at the moment of my conception, but my parents did not create my spirit. Therefore, my body, which had a beginning, will die. But my spirit, which is part of God, will have no ending, and therefore it cannot have had a beginning, any more than God had a beginning.

So the common Christian belief that we will exist with God forever forces us to take seriously the idea that we have always existed with God. And that radically alters our concept of who we are and how we fit into God's overall plan.

Satan exists to foil God's plans.

If Satan created himself, then God is not sovereign but only one of several creators. But if Satan did not create himself, who did? Who else is there but God? And if God created Satan, then Satan is not truly evil because no evil can exist in God. Therefore, Satan must be part of God's good plan. It is likely, however, that God allowed *us* to create Satan from our own fear to teach us the difference between loving and destructive behavior.

God created 2/3 of the world's population in order to send them to hell.

This is what the church would have us believe when it claims to be the only true religion. God knows everything, including how many people will never hear the good news of Jesus. To condemn them for something of which they are totally ignorant is the act of a tyrant. What about the retarded and those who are not competent to make a decision for Christ? If God makes exceptions for these people, what other exceptional categories might there be?

God gave us free will but didn't intend for us to use it.

When we blame our sinfulness on free will, we forget that our free will is a gift from God. How can it be evil if God created it? And God certainly didn't give us free will in order to tempt us to evil with it, since scripture tells us that God doesn't tempt anyone.[14] God could just as easily have created us incapable of disobedience. Why should we be punished for using a capacity which God built into us at creation? And how "free" is free will if we are punished for using it in certain ways? Being able to make choices is the only road to maturity, but it reaches its destination through the many byways of error.

If Jesus is God, then where was God while Jesus was on earth?

Obviously, Jesus was only partly God. But which part? And what percentage of God was he? Was he God when he got angry and cleansed the Temple? Was he God when he cried on the cross, "My God, why did you abandon me?"[15] If Jesus was fully God, then God can be killed. This is a very primitive conception. The spirit of God was in him, but that same spirit is in us also. So the difference between Christ and us is one of degree, not of type. He expects us to evolve and become more like him. Understanding that fact clarifies what Jesus means when he says, "[You] will do even greater things."[16]

There are many traditional beliefs such as these which do not hold up under closer scrutiny. They are holdovers from a more primitive period in church history. They all contain God's truth, but we have gotten into the habit of interpreting them literally rather than spiritually. As a result, we need to rethink them and bring them into line with more recent revelations about the nature of God. We should not be afraid to confront these inconsistencies in our belief system, because doing so forces us to get rid of some of the human projections we have used to define God. We are faced with an important choice: defending a human religion or exploring spiritual reality. My former presbytery felt that it had to do the former. Those who are hungry for the truth should have no problem choosing the latter.

I have met countless people who have had their own "aha" moment, who have said in effect, "Once I was blind but now I can see." They suddenly ran afoul of their junior high understanding of God and realized that it no longer defined the God in whom they had come to believe. Some were afraid that they would have to leave the church, but I am convinced that they should stay within their faith community and tell their story. Only when many such "heretics" unite their voices inside the church will other people be given permission to do their own thinking.

If we are serious about our spiritual quest, we may find that it will take us to places we never could have imagined in our Sunday school days. It may land us on the shore of a whole new world which we never knew existed. Losing our innocence is necessary if we are to grow up. But growing up allows us to develop a whole new kind of faith, a mature faith which is not afraid to be open to God. Unless that is our goal, then our religion is nothing more than empty form.

IV

MY KINDERGARTEN FRIEND

When I was in kindergarten, I had a best friend named Bobby who lived down the block. We were in the same class, walked to school together, played together, did overnights at each other's house, and enjoyed being pals.

Bobby's father was a lay preacher. I thought he looked like a powerful old man although he must have been all of thirty. He wore white shirts with the sleeves rolled up in careful folds so that they exposed his biceps. Bobby loved to have him bend down, "make a muscle," and watch me feel it admiringly.

Bobby was stocky and tough. I was skinny and shy. I often found myself lying on my back on the lawn with Bobby sitting on top of me claiming his superiority. He was the boss. He called the shots when we were together.

One of Bobby's favorite comments, which he often threw in my face, was, "My father can beat up your father!" I had no doubt he was right. I sometimes worried that his father might sneak into our house some night just to prove it!

Chapter 4

GOD, THE ULTIMATE CENTER

The "heretics" who are sparking the new reformation want to unhook the church from its historic tunnel vision and turn it around so it can witness what God is doing today. Part of that process, which we detailed in the last chapter, involves updating some of the elements in the Christian belief system. The primary doctrine which needs modification, and which we will discuss in this chapter, is the idea that Christianity is the only true religion.

There are multiple ways of seeing God, many religious pathways to the divine. Anna, in *Mr. God, This is Anna,* explains this by saying that we're all playing different notes in the same musical chord.[17] The heretical among us want the church to give up its chauvinistic view that it alone has the truth. When the church understands that it is one note in a divine chord, one spoke in a spiritual wheel, it will be better able to focus on God's truth rather than wasting energy on its introverted message, that there is no salvation outside the Christian belief system.

Christians criticize the first century Jews for not recognizing that God had come to them in Jesus to begin a new dispensation. The Jews were closed to that visitation because they were focused on the past, so the tide of spiritual leadership flowed away from them and broke on more welcoming shores.

The same thing is happening today. If the church fails to recognize the beginning of this new spiritual age, it will be relegated to some religious backwater. God needs an institution which is prepared to face the future, which can channel the current spiritual wave into the lives of its people. The first step is to shake off the blinders which keep it convinced that it is God's only true voice. In a modern world where empire is being destroyed and wars of national liberation are being fought, there is no room for this kind of religious imperialism, certainly not within the world's major democracy.

How did we come to think that God loves only those who claim the name of Christ? Can we reexamine this ancient belief in a way that helps us appreciate its purpose while allowing us to lovingly let it go? I believe we can. We do it by asking what we perceive as our "center."

People in Galileo's world were certain that their physical senses told them the truth. Looking toward the heavens made it obvious that the earth is the center of the universe, that it stands still while the sun revolves around it. People who disagreed with this supposed fact were considered to be "senseless"—they ignored the clear evidence of their senses.

Reliance on our senses can lead to some peculiar impressions. We watch a "motion" picture and allow our eyes to trick us into believing that the images are really in motion. We hear a sound similar to one which frightened us in the past and react in fear even when no threat is present. Chemicals in a prescribed combination can convince us that we are tasting a certain kind of fruit when in fact the food item contains no fruit at all. An early Russian cosmonaut stated that, since he did not see God while he was in orbit, God does not exist. So, although we rely on our five senses to help us interact with the world, they frequently tell us something other than the full truth.

The perception in Galileo's day, based on the evidence of the physical senses, was that the place where we stand is an unmoving center and that all of life swirls around that point. This impression is based on a reality which is common to every human being. Each one of us is the center of his own universe. Everything I do moves out into the world from that central point—me—and everything which the world does moves toward me on one of many spokes for which I provide the hub.

As I was writing this chapter, I happened to read *Hagar the Horrible* on the comic page of the local paper one night.[18] Hagar's son asks him, "Dad, if you think the world is flat, where is the exact geographical center?" And Hagar answers, "Right where I'm standing, son!" And the lad goes off thinking to himself, "Boy! Talk about your healthy egos!" It was no coincidence that that strip appeared at that moment. [See chapter 10 on Coincidence] It underlined this very point. Each one of us is the central point in his own universe.

Therefore, when I set out on a search for truth, I must remember that I have a unique point of view. The information streaming in toward me from all directions is sorted, judged and filed from that central perspective and eventually coalesces to create a worldview which is exclusively mine. And since no one is capable of standing with me in the exact center of my world, no one can tell me that my impressions are wrong. They can stand alongside me, perhaps, but no one else can stand *in* my shoes.

So, one of our most difficult tasks is to imagine ourselves at the center of someone else's universe, to view the world from an angle even slightly different from our own. Looking at things from an angle always produces some degree of distortion, and the distortion I see in someone else's position is often interpreted by me as error. How do we survive, much less create peace, in a world where everyone views everything from a different central point?

Before we attempt to answer that question, let's look at the profound ways in which this universal perception—seeing ourselves as the center—colors every stage of our growth and development. We begin as infants who feel that the universe is merely an extension of our body. Our very helplessness becomes a powerful tool. Since we cannot care for ourselves, we expect the world to drop everything when we express a need. We are born "self-centered" because this is the only way we can survive.

From that initial stage, we expand our consciousness to include our family. We tend to overlook the shortcomings of our care-givers and maximize their strengths and assets. We brag that our family is the best, the richest, the most talented, that it has the biggest house, the flashiest car, the most exceptional children. My kindergarten friend, Bobby, who boasted that "my father can beat up your father," felt that his family was the best because he was a part of it. Royalty laid claim to the "divine right of kings," the idea that its family had a God-given right to be rich and comfortable even though the masses lived in misery. So from my infant center I move to a place where I see my family as the center of my world, and I want to be the center of that family. This is why we hear the lament, "Mom always loved you more than me!"

Later we expand our circle of awareness to include a number of families, a tribe, and we are taught to see our group as central and all others as enemies. That attitude may have been necessary for survival in a tribal world, but when it carries over into religion it produces damaging distortions. The Hebrews knew God as Yahweh, their tribal deity. Their god told them that they were the "chosen" people, the most important humans on earth, the only ones who could count on Yahweh for guidance and protection. This centrist perception was so pronounced that they thought of Yahweh's power as extending only as far as the boundaries of their Hebrew land. Thus arose the concept of the "holy land," the "sacred soil." The painful and destructive consequences of that belief are still being felt today, incredibly, three thousand years later.

When tribes began to coalesce into larger groups, the rise of nationalism expanded the concept of center to include the entire country. "We are the superpower, the first nation in the world." "We have a manifest destiny to conquer." *Deutschland uber alles.* German soldiers marched into World War I wearing belt buckles which proclaimed, *Gott mit uns,* "God with us." This presumably meant that God would help them slay their enemies as God had helped the Israelites in the past. Their belief that God was on their side conveniently turned their enemies into the enemies of God.

In a larger circle of awareness, race was seen as a designation of who was in and who was out. My race, of course, was the central one, the superior one. Look at the history of apartheid in South Africa. Slaveowners in the United States rationalized their practice by debating the question of whether black men had souls. Germany bragged about being the "master race" and saw as its destiny the domination of other less developed peoples. Nazi propagandists talked about the natural inequality of the races, with Jews being on the lowest level, and used that belief to justify the "final solution."

We see clearly how blind and destructive are the theories that proclaim "I am the center of life and everyone else is peripheral to me." But we are not so clear about those areas where we still believe that we *are* the center. For instance, this centrist view of life is even played out on a cosmic plane. Many believe that we are the only intelligent life form in the universe. We see our little planet Earth as God's most unique and cherished creation. (If we truly believed that, we might take a lot better care of it!) And even among those who believe that there is other intelligent life out there, many assume that it is hostile. It is the enemy specifically because it is different. This Earth-centered belief, that we are alone in the universe, will be seen by our descendants to be as childish as the 17th century view of a stationary earth is to us.

Finally, this gives us a fresh perspective from which to look at the concept that Christianity is the one true religion. Christians have multiple reasons for this belief. One of the most telling is Jesus' statement in John 14:6: "I am the way, the truth, and the life. No one comes to the Father but by me." We will deal with this quote in Chapter 13. But none of these justifications can change the fact that thinking of my religion as the only true faith is using the same kind of prejudiced perception as all these other examples: Because it is my religion, it must be the best. This is nothing more than an adult's version of Bobby's boast: My god can beat up your god!

If Christianity is at the center of God's love and acceptance, then all other religious people, regardless of their beliefs, are pagans doomed to hell. Even within Christianity, Roman Catholics have long claimed to be "the one true church" within "the one true faith," putting Protestants and all others outside the circle of God's pleasure. If we reject elitism within our own faith, we must also disavow it with regard to the rest of the world's religions.

If we depose the Christian faith from its perch as the sole truth, what is left? How can we continue to feel secure in a religion which is just one among many different ways of understanding God? The following chapters will deal with this matter in detail. But we begin by returning to the original question: What do we perceive as our center? We must be able to see by now that all of these beliefs—that the world exists to fulfill my needs, that my father can beat up your father, that my country is always right even when it's wrong, that there is no salvation outside my faith—arise from a narrow view of life generated by fear of others. These ideas are coping mechanisms designed to give us a sense of security and belonging. And because they are human inventions, they are not a true reflection of God's loving plan.

In the following chapter, we will discuss dyads, the fact that the world comes to us in paired opposites. For instance, we are equipped with both physical vision and spiritual insight. What we discover is that a physical view of things tends to separate us while spiritual vision brings us together. The church must reexamine its claim to uniqueness because that very assertion is motivated by physical and not spiritual vision, by fear, not faith, by exclusiveness, not community. And if the chief institution of God's witness has lost its spiritual orientation and become part of the world, how can it claim to speak the truth? It is salt which has lost its savor and it will be trampled under foot.

The alternative is obvious. If my physical sight leads me to believe that I am the center of the world and superior to others, my spiritual vision shows me a higher truth. If we are all part of God, created in God's image, then there is nothing but God. And that means, of course, that God is the only true center. When I am part of God, God's center becomes my center. What do I see when I look at life from this perspective? I see that each of us is a spoke and that God is the hub. I see that we are all part of a vast and loving plan, that reality is composed of many points of view, many stories like mine, many different approaches to God, and that God cherishes them all.

When I begin to understand the full implications of making God my center, I can project this process to even larger areas. I can see on the horizon the possibility that our *inner* circle may one day expand to include all of mankind, all of nature, perhaps even all of creation.

V

THE HARPSICHORD

An old piano teacher was once visited by a former student who lived at a distance. She brought her two young children along with her, and the old man delighted in getting to know them: Alex, four, and his sister, Rachael, who was seven. Rachael had recently begun to study piano and was anxious to show her skills to her mother's former teacher.

After Rachael played several pieces, both children explored the house, examining the old man's interesting possessions. Alex wandered into a room where the teacher kept his antique harpsichord. He was astonished to see that the natural notes on the instrument were ebony and the sharps were bone, the opposite arrangement of their piano at home.

He rushed back looking for his sister and found her sitting on the piano bench, amusing herself by playing one of her pieces again. Sputtering, uncertain how to phrase his explanation, he pointed to the black sharps and said, "I saw them. They're white!"

Rachael looked at him as though he had lost his mind. "What do you mean, they're white. They're black. That's why they call them 'black notes!'"

"No!" Alex shouted. "They're white." Then, pointing to the naturals, he said, "And these are black!"

His sister merely laughed. "You're crazy, Alex! Look at them. These are white and these are black." Alex began to cry and called for his mother. When the two adults approached to see what was the matter, Rachael said sarcastically, "He's forgotten his colors again. He says the white notes are black and the black notes are white."

"They are!" Alex moaned. "I saw them." The old teacher immediately understood the problem. Taking both children by the hand, he led them into the drawing room where the harpsichord stood. Rachael's jaw dropped when she saw the instrument's keyboard and Alex, pointing in triumph, said, "See, I told you so!"

Chapter 5

THE LESSON IN DYADS

What have we said so far? We are experiencing a modern reformation; Creative thinkers are leading the way; Part of the process involves updating some outmoded religious beliefs including the idea that Christianity is the one true faith.

The overall theme of this book has to do with the contrast between religion and spirituality. These are flip sides of the same coin: religion is the physical body which houses heavenly truth, and spirituality is the soul without which religion is merely a jumble of dead rituals. Since human beings are physical/spiritual creatures, our relationship with God has both physical and spiritual dimensions: our concrete side relates more easily to the visible aspects of religion—buildings, rituals, books of theology, rules of conduct—while our soul finds its natural environment in a mystical, visionary connection to God. Both of these elements exist in everyone, but in vastly different proportions.

In the western world, we have downplayed the significance of our spiritual dimension because it seems at odds with our primarily scientific orientation. We have been taught: If you can't see it, feel it, weigh it, measure it, it isn't real. People with this orientation are uncomfortable with the idea of the spiritual world. They want to be in control; they don't like to think that we are ultimately answerable to unseen forces. This is the dilemma in which the church is caught: how can it be faithful to its tradition and answerable to God at the same time? It usually compromises by saying that God speaks to us today through the traditions of yesterday.

To understand this dynamic more clearly we need to discuss duality, the fact that the world is filled with dyads, paired opposites. Within this phenomenon we find both a model of God's plan for the universe and a possible blueprint for the church of the future.

Most of us don't like dualities, paradox. It is much easier to live in a world where things are black or white. When we are told that something is both black *and* white, we get very confused. In the physical world, we think in terms of *either/or*. But we discover, much to our consternation, that the spiritual world operates on the basis of *both/and*. God's world is filled with paradox. That's why we avoid it; we can't stand paradox. We want neat, clear-cut answers. We have mentioned some of the distinctions the church makes: Christian/non-Christian, conservative/ liberal, etc. We live in a world where we want one of those sides to be right and the other wrong. It would drive us crazy to be told that both are "right." After all, unless only one side is correct, how will we know if we are winners or losers?

Yet, we live in a world of dyads, of matched opposites, a world in which every coin has two faces, every issue two legitimate points of view. This truth applies to the universe, to ourselves, even to God. We need to realize that the dyads which exist all around us are there to teach us something essential, something without which we will never be able to find oneness with God. This is a divine mystery. God is one and we are part of God's oneness. But in our *human* form, we are the other side of God. Thus, embracing our dual nature while we are in the flesh will eventually lead to perfect unity with God when we return to spirit. This is why the church so often misses the basic message of the spiritual world. The church thinks almost exclusively in terms of *either/or's*.

What are some of the dyads with which we are surrounded? Physics has to do with the structure of the universe. But the physicist tells us that visible physical reality has a corresponding invisible, non-physical dimension. Material objects appear to be solid and tangible, yet this is an illusion; they are actually composed of organized energy—atoms and molecules. These are not physical at all, but closer to what we might call "spiritual." The irony is that the physicist must confess that his physical universe is ultimately non-physical.

So, is the universe physical or spiritual? It can be both. Is light composed of waves or particles? We have recently learned that it can be either. Is a keyboard white with black sharps or black with white sharps? Both arrangements exist and, even though they appear to be opposites, they are merely different means to the same end—creating music.

We humans are composed of two diametrically opposed elements, flesh and spirit. We refer to this union in offhand ways: "It's a struggle to keep body and soul together." "The spirit…is willing, but the flesh is weak."[19] The union of these two diverse elements makes the difference between a lively friend and a cold corpse. So, are we physical or spiritual beings? The answer is yes. We are both, even though the two are opposite states of being. Our limited human minds want to simplify the matter, to avoid the paradox by calling for an *either-or* answer. But a body without a spirit is a cadaver and a spirit without a body is a ghost. To be human is to live within the paradox.

Our brains are divided in half, with the left side leaning toward the physical and concrete while the right side contains more spiritual or abstract capabilities. In addition, our physical and spiritual natures each have their own set of senses to deal with their respective worlds. The five senses of our physical body help us interact with the physical environment. But our spiritual side is also supplied with its own special senses, among them imagination, intuition, dreams, visions, psychic powers, faith, spiritual sensitivity. Whether we perceive the universe to be physical or spiritual depends on which set of senses we use. While we are intended to use them equally, we have been conditioned to depend almost exclusively upon our physical senses. Is it any wonder that our conclusions about reality lean toward the physical side? The irony is that even the church has fallen into this trap. It is far more likely to use reason than intuition to understand God, even though it preaches that "God is Spirit, and only by the power of [God's] Spirit can people worship [God] as [God] really is."[20]

God is one and undivided, but our experience of God takes two forms. Since God is infinite spirit, often perceived to be distant and unreachable, it is difficult for finite humans to comprehend God. As a result, we find numerous ways in which to reduce God to our scale, to simplify God's transcendent reality so it will fit our limited minds. This anthropomorphic habit, most familiar in the image of God as an old man with a long white beard, is as ancient as the human race.

For Christians, Jesus of Nazareth is the physical definition of God. The Nicene Creed states that Jesus is "of one substance with the Father." So we visualize God in both spiritual and physical forms. Native American spirituality sees a connection between the Great Spirit (transcendent Father who is the creator of life) and Mother Earth (immanent nurturer who is the bearer of life). Roman Catholics balance the masculine perception of God by emphasizing God's feminine side in their veneration of the Virgin Mary. The concept of the Trinity is an admission that God cannot be described as one-dimensional. God is too richly faceted to be captured by a single term or a solitary image. But so is creation. And so are we.

This multi-dimensional God created a physical/spiritual universe. God then populated it with humans who share God's spiritual nature even while they function in what appears to be a totally material environment. And to trick us into discovering the secret of our dual nature, God has filled our life with dyads which serve as clues to what we really are. Practically everything in creation is linked in pairs. Light is opposed by non-light, darkness. Evil is the flip side of good. Every major key in music has its relative minor, every yin has its yang. *Up-down, in-out, big-little, cold-hot, happy-sad, male-female.* Life comes at us in paired opposites. These differences force us to make choices, and in those choices we move closer to God.

When we reflect on this universal structure, we immediately see the reason for its existence. We are defined by our opposites. If there were no "down," we would have no concept of "up." Light is special only because we have been frightened by the darkness. Men partially define themselves by being different from women, yet embrace the contrast in the phrase, "Vive le difference!" We say, "Every coin has two faces." Try to imagine a coin with only one face, a coin which, when you turned it over, disappeared. Impossible. Every coin has to have two sides, even if one of them is blank. The second face is necessary in order for the first to exist. Remove either one and they both disappear.

Yet, we run from the implications of all this. In our superficial approach to divinity, we continue to dice truth into bite-sized black and white chunks. We fail to see that ultimate truth is more than the sum of our little bits of understanding. As long as we focus on a black and white world, we will miss the glory of the rainbow. And that is a problem, because God lives in the rainbow.

The church is a dyad. It has both physical and spiritual dimensions. Its physical side includes a building, a congregation, a heritage, a theology, a style of life and worship. But at its spiritual level it is an association of people attempting to transcend the physical, to achieve oneness with the divine, to transform the world into a spiritual kingdom, to uncover the mystery of who we really are. The cross reminds us that truth is found in both the vertical and horizontal relationships of life, the mystical and the practical. If we take the cross apart and use only its vertical or horizontal member, it loses both its function and its meaning.

Yet, the church tends to deny its own dual nature. For one thing, its deeper purpose as a community seeking oneness with God often gets lost in the politics of managing the earthly institution. For another, it tends to identify its theology with the mind of God so that those who disagree with it are demonized. When we confront differences among believers, we seldom embrace those differences as divine dyads. We see them as personal threats and demand either/or responses. "Either you agree with our definition of faith, or we will brand you a heretic, an unbeliever, a pagan." I know this is true. It happened to me.

What this book explores is the option of turning the church into a community where differences are embraced, where the primary concern is not the politics of power but the thrill of spiritual discovery. We have a choice: we can put our energy into being "Christian," assuming that this is the only way to achieve the salvation of our souls; or we can move to a higher goal—the ultimate purpose of our faith and of every faith—living together daily in the Kingdom of God.

Let's begin by embracing the dyads which crack open the mystery of who we are. My town is composed primarily of Presbyterians and Roman Catholics. One of my friends once said to me, "So-and-so is a very nice person but, you know, she's a [whisper] Catholic!" She said it in the same tone of voice she used to report that someone had cancer. Truth is found in both Protestant *and* Catholic traditions, in both Christian *and* non-Christian religions. We need to embrace both the physical *and* the spiritual aspects of the faith, the horizontal *and* the vertical in life, the people who agree with us *and* the people who don't. Why? Because nothing exists—no idea, no tradition, no reality—which is not part of God. And since all the parts of God are good, they coordinate in some ultimate pattern at some divine level.

A certain cartoon shows an executive instructing his human resources manager, "We need to focus on diversity. Your goal is to hire people who all look different but think just like me."[21] Our temptation is to segregate ourselves into little cliques where everyone thinks the same. We struggle to achieve inclusiveness but find it incredibly difficult. Yet, the differences between us are not a reason for separation. Marriage, after all, is a relationship between two entirely different kinds of people. We maintain the institution of marriage between male and female, the ultimate human dyad, knowing that each is half of a larger entity, yet acknowledging that the essential differences between man and woman will create great love *and* great stress. We do not, however, avoid marriage or say that there is something essentially wrong with it because of its inherent difficulties.

In the 21st century, we must reunite the two halves of the spiritual dyad that is the church—the traditionalists and the visionaries, those who think like us and those who don't. We must end exclusion and see diversity of opinion as the path to wholeness. God has put us together for a reason. We are all disciples of Jesus. We need to realize that if we use only the black or the white keys, we will miss half the potential harmony.

VI

THE OCEAN

A little boy from the midwest was taken to the Atlantic coast by his parents. One of the anticipated highlights of their trip was a day at the beach. The boy had never seen the ocean before but he had heard a great deal about it. On the day they went to the shore, the weather was beautiful with bright sunshine and gentle ocean breezes. The boy played in the sand, romped in the surf and delighted in the entire experience.

When he returned home, one of his friends asked him what the Atlantic Ocean was like. He tried to describe it but it had been such an overwhelming experience that he was unable to find the right words. Finally, in frustration, he said, "Come to my house and I'll show you."

"What do you mean?" asked his friend. "How can you show me the ocean at your house?"

"I brought it home with me," the little boy explained. "It's in a bottle on a shelf in my room."

Chapter 6

RE-IMAGINING GOD

God and religion are two different matters.

That seems like an odd statement. We think of God only within a religious context. In fact, the concept of "God" defines what religion is all about. But we need to reexamine that idea.

God *IS*. Religion is merely a way of trying to understand *what* God is. Religion does not contain God any more than a bottle of seawater contains the ocean. God existed before religion was developed and God will exist long after it is no longer necessary. God *is* reality, and all the efforts of religion to define the divine do not change by one iota what God is.

Theology may not even be the proper discipline within which to hunt for clues as to the nature of God. Theology has pre-conceived notions about God and focuses on its own agenda rather than investigating whatever new evidence may become available.

Science claims that it is impossible to prove the existence of God and thus concludes that the study of God cannot be a scientific pursuit. But science investigates many things which are invisible. The wind is invisible but we can measure its effect on physical objects. Subatomic particles are invisible but we can study the way they influence other molecular entities. Pluto was invisible until the irregular movements of other heavenly bodies betrayed its existence.

God may be invisible but the effects of God's presence are all around us. Science tells us that what appears to be physical matter is actually a non-physical arrangement of pure energy. Thus the fundamental character of the visible world is closely related to that of the spiritual world, separated only by a difference in vibration rates. It is as essential to understand our non-physical source as it is to study the sun which gave birth to our solar system. And science may be able to do this more objectively than religion.

43

Yet, we do not make the study of the spiritual world a priority, we do not look at it in the same disciplined, objective way that we examine the heavens. We are convinced that there is an unbridgeable void between those two worlds, that the physical is "real" and the spiritual is illusory. Ironically, just the opposite is true—the physical is transitory and the spiritual is permanent and therefore "real."

So we cherish our little bottle of seawater, thinking that we have captured the ocean. But we cannot make infinity fit our small spaces. We have to go seek it, dare to plunge into its depths. That choice is so daunting, however, that we opt for the safer alternative. We bring home a dram of God which we keep in a theological container on our ecclesiastical shelf, and we use it to convince ourselves that we know all there is to know about the divine.

It is said that the work of childhood is play. In play, children experiment with grown-up situations by reducing them to child-sized games and investigating what it feels like to engage in those activities. If we look closely at these theological efforts of ours, they reveal that we are still in the childhood of our spiritual development, playing safe little games with the eternal.

The issue is one of control. We are afraid to give God total control of our lives for fear that God might demand of us something costly and challenging. And so we try to retain control by telling God just how far we are willing to be led. We justify this process by developing a theology which permits us to stay within our comfort level. And then we claim that God has ordered us not to go beyond those limits!

To end that game we need to grow up spiritually. How do we do that? Episcopal Bishop John Spong once said that if horses had gods, they would look like horses. Someone else has made the observation that God created humankind in God's image, and then we turned around and returned the compliment. We insist on worshipping a God small enough to fit the confines of our human intelligence.

We cannot begin to move into mature spirituality until we give up this human image of God, until we understand what J. B. Phillips meant when he warned us, *Your God Is Too Small*. This process begins when we confront one of faith's major paradoxes: There is an infinite chasm between God and ourselves, but at the same time we are intimately connected. What does that mean?

It means that there is nothing but God. Nothing exists outside of God, not Satan, not creation, not ourselves, not the Holocaust, not the entire realm of heaven. That fact is so fundamental and yet so unsettling that most people stop right there.

But God does not have a warehouse stocked with human limbs and organs for use in assembling new bodies. Nor does God share eternity with a diabolical clone whose job it is to create evil events that frustrate all of God's plans. Nothing exists outside of God and therefore creation is composed of God's own substance. Everything in creation, at its most basic level, is filled with the essence of God. *There is nothing else.*

It's like the connection between the power plant fifty miles away and the light bulb in the lamp next to your favorite chair. The lamp, the household wiring, the high tension lines, the power plant itself are all secondary, all merely part of a delivery system. The invisible energy produced by the generators flows through those lines, and it is that energy which heats the filament in your light bulb and illuminates the words in your book. The hardware is dead without the energy which flows through it. The only difference is that at its source the power is rated at a million megawatts and in your light bulb it is stepped down to a mere hundred watts.

Just so, God and we are part of the same energy system. I may be as tiny compared to God as my light bulb is compared to the generator's output, but the same energy flows through both of us. That is what God meant by saying, "Let us make man in our image."[22] That is what Jesus meant when he said, "The Father and I are one."[23]

Now, having said that, we have to recognize the opposite truth, that the difference between my little light bulb and a megawatt power station is enormous. The station may power my bulb, but if it were to shoot *all* its power my way it would not only explode my little bulb, it would burn down my house and most of my neighborhood. That power has to be stepped down through a series of transformers in order to be useable at my level. Those transformers do their job so well that the power of the station is completely tamed and comes to me in a trickle which my system is able to utilize safely.

The same thing is true with God. God's power flows through me, surrounds me, energizes me and gives my life vitality and imagination. But as it comes my way, it has to be stepped down so that it doesn't totally overwhelm me. Different people receive this power at different frequencies. Those who receive it at a higher voltage exhibit certain traits which seem unusual—psychic powers, healing skills, spiritual wisdom, and so on. But in every case the transformer steps that power down from a divine frequency to a human one. To broaden the image, if God is 100-dimensional and we are merely three-dimensional creatures, then we cannot conceive of anything beyond those three dimensions. We even have trouble trying to fit time into our awareness as a fourth dimension, so imagine how impossible it would be to understand the 43rd or the 87th dimension of God.

Thus, God's energy is stepped down until it reaches us at a three-dimensional rate, changing everything that comes to us into a mode which we can understand. As a result, we see God as a three-dimensional reality, with all the characteristics and failings of our three-dimensional world.

But, this humanoid deity of scripture, characterized by anger, punishment, warlikeness and jealousy in addition to love and forgiveness, fails to show us the true nature of God. To recover a more accurate image of God, we must step outside our three-dimensional heritage and go through a reverse series of transformers, increasing the voltage of our understanding. This is the function of faith. Ironically, the church has never learned to do this very well. It is still reading the truth of God by the light of a 100-watt bulb. What it tells us is not untrue, but that feeble light leaves a lot of the truth in darkness.

So, what is the true nature of God? I wish I could give you the answer! But I too am limited by a three-dimensional mind. I don't have the definitive answer any more than the next person. Everyone has his own idea. Little Anna, in the sequel to *Mister God, This is Anna,* explains the nature of God this way: You can't see something big like a mountain up close. You have to get far away from it to see it all. But you can't ever get far enough away from God to see him. He's too close. That's why he's invisible.[24]

We need to find a way of representing God which is more profound than the old man in the clouds with the lengthy beard. The new millennium calls for new images which, although they may not be technically correct, can nudge our minds out of the old ruts and move us a little closer to the truth.

What alternate images can we use to describe God?

Perhaps a vast power plant with lines running to every human heart feeding not only energy but love into our souls.

Or an ocean of infinite depth, composed not of water but of a loving and creative personality in which every drop is a soul both distinct from and yet part of the vastness called the sea.

The universe itself is a model for God. The billions of celestial bodies represent all the conscious entities in creation, each one free to operate in its own orbit, yet held in a precise and expanding relationship with the whole.

A friend of mine feels that God is creating a divine consort, a soul-mate, and that each of us is a cell in an enormous spiritual organism which will one day be in full communion with God.

Now, while I don't pretend that any of these descriptions is literal, they do go beyond the usual three-dimensional images which we were taught in Sunday School. And if we can get away from the old man image, we can also move beyond the idea of an angry, punishing God who created us imperfect, yet demands perfection, and whose justice requires that all those who belong to the wrong religion end up in hell.

We have all heard the story of the blind men who felt an elephant and came up with descriptions as diverse as a wall, a spear and a tree. We are blind people trying to feel the face of an unseen God. What our spiritual fingers tell us often depends on where we live in the world. One person may feel a God who is intimately involved with creation, while another senses a God who is distant and indifferent to the suffering of mankind. A third may encounter a God who speaks of the possibility of human perfection, while a fourth finds a tyrant anxious to punish every infraction of the spiritual law. Others feel a God who requires varying types of diet, methods of prayer, styles of worship. Still others claim that the God they "see" demands faith healing, meditation, alms-giving, celibacy, snake-handling, speaking in tongues, perpetual silence.

Who is right? They are all right. And they have all missed the point. Any method which helps an individual find God is useful. Yet it is not through ritual and cultic behavior that we discover our deepest purpose. The Bible tells us to "Be still, and know that I am God."[25] Ultimately our spiritual quest can be satisfied only by discovering the spark of God which is inside ourself. And when we learn that God is not "up there" but that each of us is part of God, we discover the truth at the heart of every religion: We are all brothers and sisters; loving our neighbor is loving ourself; and we are absolutely loved and embraced by God despite our differences and self-doubt.

VII

THE FENCE

Religion and The Kingdom of God exist on different sides of the same fence. The fence serves to separate time from eternity. As we move along our earthly pilgrimage on this side of the fence, God keeps pace with us in eternity, out of sight on the other side.

From our side of the fence we can only imagine what exists in that other dimension. People walking along with us are full of rumors about what's over there. They tell us of people who have looked over, of beings from that side who have appeared to them, of documents which explain the reality of life on the far side of the fence. But for the most part, we do not know what is hidden by that barrier.

Except...once, long ago, there was a break in the fence. An opening appeared and through that opening walked a man named Jesus. He came through from that mysterious other side and tried to explain what exists there. He promised that there would be other openings in the fence at various intervals along our journey and that he would continue to visit us to tell us more about life on his side. Most of all, he assured us that our faith in him would eventually make the fence transparent.

But as time went on and we walked along on our side, farther from that ancient opening, many people began to doubt what he had said. Most came to believe that there was only that one hole in the fence and that there would never be any others. They insisted that in order to know anything about the other side, we would have to go back to that old opening. They claimed that it was safer to rely on the one gap we knew about than to hope for future openings which might never materialize.

The problem was that, when they went back to the opening, they found no one on the other side. There was merely a note which said, "I am with you always. Look for me on the other side of the fence wherever you are at the moment."

Many people have poked their heads through the fence in what they call Near-Death Experiences. Others have spoken of their ability to make the fence dissolve by faith. But the difficulty is that we can't do that for each other. Every person must learn that skill for himself.

And so the fence remains between us. Some tell us there is nothing on the other side. Others say that God is exactly opposite us and speaks to us regularly if we are willing to listen. The most religious among us keep going back to the old opening and reporting that they don't hear anything new. And together we make so much noise on this side that it is difficult to hear what's going on on the other.

Chapter 7

RELIGION AND THE KINGDOM OF GOD

Jesus of Nazareth was not a Christian.

That seems like an obvious statement. But there is a real question as to whether he intended *us* to become "Christians" after he was gone. He did not come to found a new religion. On the contrary, his ministry was an announcement that the time for religion had ended, that the Kingdom had arrived. Later on, others who misunderstood his message created a new cult around his teachings because they did not know how to be spiritual without being religious. Jesus probably would not have been pleased.

Religion began in a superstitious period of pre-history when our primitive forebears realized that a power beyond their control could make life easy or miserable. Rain, fertile soil, successful crops, destructive storms, even the sunrise were in the hands of some invisible force. They named that force "god." Noticing that all of these issues seemed to originate in the space over their heads, they deduced that this god must live in the sky. They concluded that he sent blessings when he was pleased and vice versa, so they sought ways to keep him happy. Thus began the phenomenon of religious behavior.

The heritage of those primitive ideas still echoes, incredibly enough, in modern religious thought and practice. The Old Testament recounts instances when the Israelites did something to displease God and God responded by turning away from them and letting them twist in the wind of their own unfaithfulness. Deut. 30:19-20 sums up this dual nature of God: "I am giving you the choice between life and death, between God's blessing and God's curse."

So, despite the refinements in thinking which had taken place since the days of the caveman, one religious attitude persisted: In order to be blessed, you had to obey God. If you disobeyed God, you would be cursed. We are so accustomed to this view of God that we no longer see it as primitive and unworthy of true divinity.

51

We would expect that Christianity, which prides itself on being the final step in religious development, has rid itself of this ancient view of God. Unfortunately, it has not. Paul wrote in Romans 6:23, "The wages of sin is death, but the free gift of God is eternal life in Christ Jesus our Lord." [RSV] The gospel of John even quotes Jesus as saying, "I am the way...; no one comes to the Father, but by me."[26] The church has interpreted this verse to mean that only Christians will be found in heaven. So the Christian faith not only concurs with the Old Testament belief that God blesses or curses us based on our behavior, but worships a God who threatens with eternal punishment those who have the bad judgment to pick the wrong religion!

Even a casual understanding of these beliefs indicates that we have not moved very far from primitive forms of religion: we still fear divine retribution, hold placating rituals, beg the heavens for our basic needs, confess our unworthiness, and offer sacrifices. All of this indicates that we look upon God as a divine tyrant who holds us hostage with the superior power of the spirit world. We may disagree with this assessment, but when we begin to deny any of these statements the whole fabric of religion, and especially of the Christianity with which we are familiar, begins to unravel.

Religion began in ignorance about God. Jesus came to tell us the truth about God. If ignorance about God gave birth to religion, then knowledge of the truth about God should make it unnecessary. But those who shaped Christian theology and practice could not grasp Jesus' clear intention to move his followers from religion into the Kingdom of God. So, rather than ending religion, they created a new one; rather than seeing the Kingdom as a spiritual fellowship, they claimed it was the religio-political establishment which they controlled and to which everyone else had to submit; instead of searching for the meaning of what Jesus called the Good News, they simply modified the old news. And disregarding Jesus' clear promise to tell us much more, they closed off debate and ignored future revelations by the Spirit.

I believe that Jesus had none of this in mind. Although he practiced his own religion, he was not a very committed Jew. This was not because he was trying to create a new, more authentic religion but because he was opposed to the politics of all religion. He broke the Sabbath, defied the leadership, desecrated the Temple and taught things contrary to the Law. Everything he did indicated his refusal to remain within the religious constraints of his own faith.

So, it is highly unlikely that Jesus was planning to fix religion by inventing a new one. What he came to say was something like:

The time of ignorance is past. God is not the enemy. He is ready to lavish on you the riches of heaven if you have the faith to receive them. Because God is so close to you, the Kingdom is in your midst. Religion merely teaches you to hope that the Kingdom will come some day. But I have come to tell you that the Kingdom has already arrived, it is here, and you have been invited to live together within it. Therefore, you can dispense with religion because it no longer has any purpose.

What he was *not* saying was that God is a demanding, distant judge who requires perfection and who rewards anything less with eternal punishment. Some may wish he had said this, may even put these words in his mouth, but when the record is examined closely I do not think it supports that point of view. Let's look at the earliest account of his teaching, the gospel of Mark. What do we find there?

Interestingly, we read nothing about sin and salvation, about God's judgment, about the rules that define a new religion. What we discover is a description of life in the Kingdom of God.

A major theme in Mark is healing, healing of the spirit as well as the body. Jesus seems to think of sin as spiritual illness which needs to be cured rather than as moral failure which needs to be punished. This is made very clear in 2:5 where, during his healing of the paralyzed man brought by four friends, he says to the paralytic, "Your sins are forgiven." The Pharisees are outraged and charge him with blasphemy. He responds, "Is it easier to say to this paralyzed man, 'Your sins are forgiven,' or to say, 'Pick up your mat and walk'?" What he means is: Since none of you can do either, who is to say that a person with one ability doesn't also have the other? He drives this point home in the next verse: "I will prove to you that the Son of Man has authority on earth to forgive sins," and he does so by healing the *physical* problem suffered by the paralyzed man. Apparently, he sees no difference between illnesses of the flesh and of the spirit. And, since he treats physical sickness with love and compassion rather than condemnation, he does the same with illness of the spirit, what we call sin.

This connection between the physical and spiritual aspects of health is further highlighted by his comments to several people following their healing. When the woman with severe bleeding touches the hem of his cloak, Jesus says to her in 5:34, "Your faith has made you well. Be healed of your trouble." Her faith is a spiritual reality, yet it has the power to affect her physical condition. And, interestingly, Jesus takes no credit for the healing. It happened as a result of her desire to be well and her belief in him. The same thing occurs in 10:52. Bartimaeus comes to him, desperate for help. We note that Jesus doesn't automatically heal him, doesn't even ask, "Do you want me to restore your vision?" Rather, he asks, "What do you want me to do for you?" He doesn't know yet what request Bartimaeus has in mind, and he can only give the man what his faith has prepared him to receive. The blind man asks for his vision to be restored and Jesus responds, without touching him, spitting or even praying as he had in previous cases, "Go, your faith has made you well." We must conclude that Bartimaeus' recovery was due largely to his own positive attitude and, perhaps, to a potential for self-healing which we all possess.

Jesus makes this even more evident in 9:23 when a man brings him his son who is possessed by an evil spirit. The father says, "Help us, if you possibly can!" Jesus throws the challenge right back to him. "Yes," he says, "if you yourself can! Everything is possible for the person who has faith." The major responsibility for the healing lies with the father, not with Jesus despite his awesome powers. This is further demonstrated in 6:5-6 where we read, "[Jesus] was not able to perform any miracles there (Nazareth)…because the people did not have faith."

In all of this, Jesus is giving us an insight into the nature of life in the Kingdom and contrasting it with ordinary religious practice. People look to religion because they believe that its hierarchy—God, institution, priest—possesses spiritual powers not granted to lay people. But by presiding over these healings recounted in Mark, both physical (hemorrhage, withered hand) and spiritual (demons), Jesus is telling us something new about the power of faith. Not only can we be healed of physical ailments by the power of faith but, he says by inference,

If you don't need a physician for your bodily illnesses, neither do you need religion for your spiritual ones. When you arrive at your destination, you no longer need directions on how to get there. The Kingdom is the destination; religion is merely a roadmap. But, the Kingdom is here. Your journey is over. Therefore, it is time to turn away from your sins and believe the Good News—God is in your midst; people are being healed; sins are being forgiven; peace is being established. So, come, be part of God's Kingdom!

Being in the Kingdom is being conscious of our oneness with God. Sin, on the other hand, is characterized by thinking of ourselves as separate from God. But religion teaches us that we *are* separate from God, separated by our human sinfulness. It tells us that Christ is of the same substance as God but that we are a different class of being, inferior and unworthy, who deserve eternal punishment. By reinforcing this sense of separation, the church teaches us to think and act like sinners. As a result, it then becomes necessary for the church to devise some redemptive act to save us from the very condition into which its theology has forced us. This is not good news!

The Good News which Jesus announced tells us the opposite story. God is our lover/creator. God made us from God's own substance in the same way that our children are made from our substance. Because of this, there is no estrangement and thus no need for a savior. We confess that we are ignorant, as all children are ignorant, that we need to grow up spiritually. But we do not give birth to our children in order to kill them if they are not perfect. We give them life in order to love them, to educate them, to nourish and support them, and to set them loose in the world to experience their independent dreams. When we do this, we discover that they have marvelous gifts to give us. God does the same thing with us. This is the actual Good News.

This contrast defines the gulf between religion and the Kingdom of God. Their differing messages are a divine dyad. The physical side of the dyad, based on our ignorance and fear, says, "God will condemn you if you are not perfect." The spiritual side of that dyad, based on knowledge and love, says, "God is, and therefore you are. Rest in the certainty that you are absolutely loved forever!" This is the essential difference between the two. Religion serves as an incubator for spirituality, but we are not meant to remain in the incubator forever.

In the Kingdom we discover that, since we are part of God, we no longer have to beg God for everything we need. Because we possess God's image we are, in a sense, like God. This means that all of God's power and resources are available to us. When we understand this, some of Jesus' statements make much more sense: "Everything is possible for the person who has faith."[27] "When you pray and ask for something, believe that you have received it, and you will be given whatever you ask for."[28] When we doubt our worthiness to receive God's gifts, our doubt clogs our receptors. To be in the Kingdom means to have no doubt about God's love and providence. This is why Jesus could perform miracles. Those who still question their worthiness need religion to help them overcome their lack of faith in God.

When you contrast these two points of view, it is easy to see that Jesus was calling for a change in our thinking: an end to the age of religion and the beginning of a new age, a Kingdom age. In the gospel of Mark, Jesus reaches out to those whom religion has rejected. He says that the old religious wineskins need to be replaced since they cannot contain his spiritual message; he explains in parables how the Spirit grows inside the hearts of people if they are not limited by their religious traditions; and he punctures the pride of the religious elite by insisting that the first will be last, that it takes childlikeness to get into the Kingdom. His anti-religious slant is plain to see.

The exception is found in 16:16 where it says, "Whoever believes and is baptized will be saved; whoever does not believe will be condemned." But this verse is contained in a conclusion which was probably not part of the original manuscript. Its addition at a later time is evidence of an early move to turn the Kingdom teachings into the dogma of a new religion. Mark was written sometime around AD 70, almost two generations after the resurrection. The other three gospels, probably written ten to twenty years later than Mark, took much of his material and added religious concepts which had developed in the interim. It is difficult to distinguish between what Jesus said and what others later claimed he said in order to give support to their new religion. But we are more likely to find the original flavor of Jesus' teaching in Mark than in the later gospels. And in Mark we find healing, not judgment, forgiveness, not condemnation, and we find a rejection of religious tradition, not support for it.

Jesus' statement in John 16:12-13—"I have much more to tell you, but now it would be too much for you to bear. When...the Spirit comes...he will lead you into all the truth"—proves that, in his opinion, religion and the Kingdom are incompatible. He is saying that the Kingdom is a dynamic reality that, although it is here among us, is still in the process of coming. It will never be fully revealed and thus no religion can ever fully contain it.

How do we change Christianity from a closed to an open system? We begin by realizing that God is not back at the old opening in the fence waiting for us to return. What would be the point of that? God created us for growth and we can only grow as we continually move forward. When we plant ourselves opposite that old opening, or keep interrupting our journey to go back for a visit, we frustrate God's clear will for us and cripple our own journey. If God's purpose for us is ever-increasing spiritual wisdom, it makes sense to believe that God is moving along with us on our spiritual pilgrimage, only inches away on the other side of the fence. When we know that God is there, anxious to speak to us and guide us and be our companion, it makes the trip much more exciting. And fruitful. And that knowledge assures us that God will constantly have new truths to reveal to us.

Those who want to move from the incubator to the Kingdom will always face the malice of well-intentioned people who think they are defending God. But making that move is the only way to spiritual freedom, and those who blaze the trail will open the way for everyone else.

VIII

LINDA'S FIRST CHRISTMAS

Our oldest daughter, Linda, was born in October. So she was fourteen months old before she could truly experience Christmas. She was fascinated by the preparations and the decorations, and thrilled by the colorful Christmas tree which stood in one corner of the dining room. She knew Santa was coming and, as gifts from family members and the congregation took their place daily under the tree, her excitement grew.

Christmas morning arrived and it was finally time to open the presents. We watched to see how our firstborn would react to all these wonderful new toys and clothes.

We were a bit startled, therefore, when she ripped off the pretty paper and ribbon, tossed the less colorful boxes in the corner, and played with the wrappings.

Chapter 8

THE CHURCH

The Christian church has a bad case of narcissism.

And that's a tragedy because it's supposed to be in love with God, not with itself. But that is one of the problems with religion. It inevitably creates its own support system and ends up spending so much time and energy on its packaging that it tends to forget what is supposed to be inside.

Contrast the first-century Christian house-meetings with St. Peter's basilica in Rome. The early Christians were not interested in where they met—they sometimes gathered secretly in tombs. They had a burning desire to share with each other what God had done in their lives since they last met and to become vessels for the Spirit's power. They felt a passionate connection with each other and a powerful sense of God's presence among them. So they came together to celebrate God and to care for each other, even at risk of their lives. Their focus was entirely on the Spirit which dwelt within.

But, sadly, when the faith gained legitimacy in the fourth century, this changed. Church leaders became preoccupied with the concerns of the physical world. Politics, possessions, and power began to displace love as the church's chief motivation.

How do we regain the church's original spiritual passion?

Let's review what we have said so far. Reexamining some of the church's doctrines creates the "heretics" who are leading the modern reformation. They want to reopen discussion on a number of topics: Christianity as the one true faith, ancient images of God, the relationship between religion and spirituality, how the church can balance tradition and revelation and still retain its integrity. Let's consider how the church must change if it is to participate in this new reformation.

As I was preparing to write this chapter, an article appeared in the local paper.[29] It told of a young girl who suffers from celiac disease which causes her to get sick from eating gluten, a protein in wheat and other grains. She is, however, able to eat rice with no problem. When her parents tried to make arrangements for her to have her first communion in the Roman Catholic church, the Archdiocese of Boston informed them that the church could not substitute a rice communion wafer for the traditional wheat one. A spokesman for the church explained, "This is not an arbitrary sort of thing, and we're talking about a religious sacrament. Bread is central to the Eucharist because of the imagery of scripture, because of the prayers of the Christian community going back thousands of years." In 1994 the Vatican issued rules for all bishops to follow. Among them was the statement that special hosts not containing gluten are invalid for the celebration of the Eucharist. One parish priest commented, "We many are sharing one bread and becoming one with Christ. We can't make different flavors for different folks and maintain that theological reality." The article concluded by noting that the girl's parents joined the Methodist Church as a result of this situation so that their daughter could participate in the sacrament of communion.

That story filled me with indignation. It's an example of the church being in love with itself. That kind of behavior is superstition, not faith. How can people talk about becoming one with Christ when they would rather exclude a child than try to accommodate her in a fellowship which they claim is based on Jesus' love? I'm quite certain that Jesus would be appalled at some of the things that are done in his name. We wonder if those in charge have ever read the scriptures they claim to be following. Jesus warns us, "If anyone should cause one of these little ones to lose his faith in me, it would be better for that person to have a large millstone tied around his neck and be drowned in the deep sea."[30] "Watch out for the [bishops], who like to walk around in their long robes and be greeted with respect in the marketplace, who choose the reserved seats in the [Cathedral] and the best places at feasts. They take advantage of [children] and rob them of their [right to worship], and then make a show of saying long prayers. Their punishment will be all the worse!"[31]

Is anyone paying attention? We are supposed to love people and use things. But in cases like this, when we put tradition above the welfare of human beings, we are guilty of loving things and using people! How can we not see the hypocrisy in this kind of behavior? This is not Christianity. It is an abuse of power by people whose position has gone to their head. Do we really believe that God cares if we *ever* go to church? God's first question when we meet on that final day will not be, "How many times did you miss mass?" It will be something like, "How much did you love? How much did you learn? In what ways did you help the Kingdom to come on earth?" Remember Jesus' warning: "Not everyone who calls me 'Lord, Lord' will enter the Kingdom of heaven, but only those who do what my Father in heaven wants them to do."[32] I cannot see how excluding a child from the sacrament is what the Father wants us to do. (See Mt. 19:14).

THE CHURCH

But the fault is not only on the Roman Catholic side of the church aisle. A Washington Post article in June, 2000 reported on the Southern Baptist Convention's (SBC) move to ban women pastors. The article stated that in 1984 the Rev. Kelly Sisson became the first woman to preach in the chapel at New Orleans Theological Seminary, which is run by the SBC. The following Sunday, a local pastor pronounced the chapel's pulpit "demonically possessed" because a woman had been allowed to preach there. Shortly afterward, delegates at the annual meeting of the SBC passed a resolution discouraging the ordination of women for "pastoral functions and leadership roles." A spokesman said, "We believe that the office of pastor is reserved to men as qualified by scripture."

Scripture was written in a time when women were considered chattel, the property of men. How can we, with straight faces, claim to base our religious behavior on moral standards which are two millennia out of date? Shall we go back to the practices of jailing debtors, hanging pickpockets, cutting the hands off of thieves and burying wives alive with their dead husbands? Someone has to blow a whistle here and wake the rest of us up. This is not acceptable behavior! The Southern Baptists are discounting half the human race. They have confused bigotry with the will of God.

Whew! Now that I've vented my sanctimonious moral outrage, let me put the hat on the other side of my head. Although I obviously do not agree with either of these actions by the organized church, I fully support the right of people to do these things. The archbishop and the SBC are not trying to destroy the church. They are operating from a sincere and historically legitimate effort to be obedient to God. And we need to respect that, whether we agree with them or not.

If what has been said in previous chapters is anything more than words, we need to consider the meaning of *centers* and *dyads* in this case. The first part of this chapter was written with the view that I am the center of my world, that my logic is so clear and my position so unassailable that everyone should agree with me. It's good to be certain of our ground, but destructive when we use our opinions to flog those who disagree with us. After all, the Baptists and the Roman Catholics are as convinced of their position as I am of mine. But merely hunkering down in our own centers means civil war. The only way to avoid that conflict is to look for a larger center.

That larger center becomes apparent when we realize that we are discussing a divine dyad here, a theological disagreement in which each side needs the other. Our own case would be much weaker without the opposing point of view. We marry a spouse whose qualities contrast with our own and whose differences help us to grow in the specific areas where we are weakest. In exactly the same way, we are married in the church—as well as in every other area of life—to partners whose thinking is diametrically opposed to our own. This is not an accident. These dyads make certain that all the various positions are covered. My desire for inclusiveness would have no focus if I could not point to some element in the church that was militating for exclusiveness. And their desire for purity of doctrine and faithfulness to tradition is strengthened by the perception that I am attempting to dismantle the ancient standards.

The True Church cannot be found in any one of its splintered elements. These fragments are created by our tendency to withdraw into barricaded compounds composed of people who think as we do. This means we talk only to people who agree with us, and in so doing we avoid being challenged. But if God's will is for us to grow in grace and in knowledge of Jesus, these enclaves are counterproductive. We need to learn that we can be part of the same fellowship and still disagree with each other. The church will never be fully mature until it embraces the full range of beliefs—the black *and* the white, the physical *and* the spiritual, the traditional *and* the innovative. We look at the Middle East and wonder why the combatants can't lay aside millennia of hostility for the privilege of living together in peace in the present. But we fail to see that that very question applies with equal relevance to us within the church.

A Christmas present usually consists of the gift and the paper and ribbon used to decorate it. Perhaps the wrapping can fool a one-year-old but it ought not to confuse an adult. We should know the difference between essence and elaboration. Religion also consists of both content and packaging. The content, the gift, is Jesus' command in Mark 12: "You shall love the Lord your God with all your heart, soul, mind and strength. And you shall love your neighbor as yourself." The packaging is the theological/institutional context that has grown up around that gift in the past two millennia. If the gift of love becomes secondary to the legalism in which it is packaged, then we demonstrate no more wisdom than Linda did at fourteen months of age.

That is not to say that the wrapping is unimportant. It adds great beauty to the gift. But while we need to nurture both, we should remember which of the two is discarded after the present is opened. Some of us are interested in taking care of the church's body while others prefer to nurture its soul. In that way, together, we make certain that the institution survives. We should be grateful to the others for attending to those aspects of the faith which we have neither the desire nor the talent to perform.

I was both taken aback and amused recently when, as a guest musician in a local Roman Catholic church, I made a comment to the choir just as the mass began. I was instantly shushed quite vigorously by several members of the group. As a fairly well-known pastor in the area, I was shocked by what seemed to be rudeness on their part, until I realized that they were equally shocked by what they perceived as rudeness on my part, especially since I *was* a pastor! As I reflected on that incident, I appreciated a quality they possessed which we Protestants for the most part have lost—reverence for sacred space. They have a concrete understanding of what scripture means when it says, "Be still, and know that I am God."[33]

But then the members of the congregation turned around and exhibited the other side of their religious sensitivity. Our group played a bell choir number during the offertory. The congregation had never before heard a bell choir perform and had invited us because they were considering forming a choir of their own. They listened in absolute silence as the sound of the bells reverberated from the stone walls of their lovely sanctuary. It was a moving and holy moment, and we were all touched. When we finished, there was a moment of silence and then the entire congregation, moved by the Spirit, broke into spontaneous applause. In the middle of the mass! It shocked everyone, not least the people who found themselves clapping in church. The priest later told us in amazement that nothing like that had ever happened in his church before. So the earlier shushing and the later ovation were another dyad, a way of making each of those experiences more meaningful

Thus, we have two approaches within the church: a routine based on scripture, and an evolving belief and practice based on the Holy Spirit's current revelations. Some would say that this is a choice between order and chaos. God speaks with one voice through tradition, but with many voices through modern revelation. Which approach is correct? Both are necessary, but no one person or group can do both. So, ironically, it requires everyone, working together, to get it all done.

We have to decide whether we want to view Christianity as a classroom-based history lesson, or as a hands-on field trip during which we look for artifacts to expand our knowledge of God. Both are essential to a good education. We may choose one path, but we need to leave room for those who want to walk the other.

Thinking of religion as elementary school and the Kingdom of God as high school reminds us that we are meant to grow spiritually rather than staying forever at the same level of understanding. As a result, the church needs to offer a variety of curricula. Or, as the writer of the letter to the Hebrews says, "Anyone who has to drink milk is still a child....Solid food, on the other hand, is for adults."[34] Too often the church has forced everyone to drink spiritual milk. But more and more people today are begging for solid food.

IX

THE INDIAN

The man was terrified. He was in the heart of a small hill, standing in a narrow crevice. The fault opened about fifteen feet over his head and also off to his right where it led out onto level ground. The gap in which he was standing was about three feet wide, and he had run into it desperately seeking to escape his pursuers. He flattened himself against the back wall trying to be invisible. His dark skin blended with the red rock of the surrounding hills, and for a moment he thought he was safe.

Suddenly, he was washed by a new wave of terror as the shadow of a man appeared on the wall facing him. He knew the man was standing on top of the little hill, searching for him. He pressed even harder against the wall, knowing that from that overhead position he could easily be seen. But it was too late.

Arrows flew in through the opening off to his right. He was immediately struck, but before he could feel any pain or shock, he slid smoothly out of his body. Rising swiftly, he emerged from the top of the opening and found himself hovering over the scene. He could see the man who had cast the shadow standing at the top of the fault, as well as the enemy warriors shooting arrows into the narrow space. And he could see his own body sprawled on the rocky floor. As he watched, the warriors ran into the opening and began kicking and stomping on his prone body, whooping as they celebrated their victory.

He acted without thinking. Only vaguely aware that he was dead, not even questioning the fact that he was suspended in midair, he felt only rage at the way these people were treating his body. His anger propelled him down among the noisy warriors, shouting, "This is not an honorable way to treat another human being. I may be your enemy but I am still a man. You would not want others to treat your body this way, whether you were dead or alive."

But they could neither hear nor see him. As far as they knew, he was only a corpse lying at their feet.

Chapter 9

MY FORMER LIFE

I was the Native American who died in that rocky crevice.

That incident was fatal in two respects: it ended my former life as an Indian, and the memory of it ended my former career as a Presbyterian minister.

Let me retrace the steps of my conversion into heresy.

When I came to western Pennsylvania in 1961, I was a "good" orthodox, conservative, doctrinaire Presbyterian pastor, and I fit right into the conservative scene which surrounded me. If someone had told me that God, with a quirky sense of humor, had brought me here to radicalize me, I would not have been amused. For almost twenty years I served my parish, uncritically doing what I was told and preaching everything that church doctrine taught.

Then, in the late 1970s, I encountered a church member who believed in reincarnation and who wanted to discuss it with me. I brushed off her ideas rather abruptly, telling her that it was an eastern concept that had no place in Christianity. We believe in the resurrection, I informed her, and the two are incompatible. In time, we entrenched ourselves behind our divergent opinions and occasionally joked with each other about the subject: I called her a heretic and she labeled me close-minded. Talk about divine humor!

Then four events happened in rapid succession.

• In mid-1979, a woman whom I had known since she was a child in my congregation stopped by for a visit. She "just happened" to leave me several books by Edgar Cayce, "the sleeping prophet," about whom I knew nothing. Reading the material introduced me to his ideas about reincarnation.

• Later in 1979, another woman came in for counseling, and in the course of our work spoke to me about a faculty member at a nearby university with whom she was working. He was doing research into past life regression as a tool for helping cancer patients learn how to become active in their own healing.

- A cousin of mine visited us in January, 1980, and left me a book by Ruth Montgomery which discussed reincarnation in great detail.

- The next month, I met the professor mentioned above, and we entered into a long friendship during which we explored much that could be termed "mystical," including his research into past lives and his discoveries about reincarnation.

I was still on the fence about the whole subject, since there was no way I could fit it into my traditional theology. It still seemed "eastern," alien and superstitious. Then, almost exactly a year later, I had a spontaneous past death recall. I suddenly and unexpectedly remembered my death as a Native American. Even though I now believe that God had carefully prepared me for the event, I was not pleased by the memory and at first tried to ignore it. I told myself it was a dream, it was my imagination, it was nonsense. But it wouldn't go away.

I could recall it in vivid detail. It had an entirely different quality than a dream; in fact it was almost more real than "real" life. I phoned my psychic faculty friend and asked him to investigate this experience for me. He called back and asked, "Do you have any birthmarks?" I told him I have a small round mark on the left side of my abdomen. He said, "From what I can learn, the recall is factual and was brought to you because you're ready for it. And the birthmark is probably a psychic memory of where you were hit by an arrow."

All of this was overwhelming at the time. I began an intensive period of reading about near-death and out-of-body experiences, about new thought and modern spirituality. One of the things I discovered was that my experience was not unusual and that it agreed with the norm in its details. Also, people who have had this kind of experience report that they know it is not just their imagination because it feels more real than "real" life, which was precisely how I had described it.

I had two choices. I could accept the memory and perhaps cause professional problems for myself. Or I could play it safe, turn my back on the experience and go on with my career. I knew that the memory was real. I believed that God wanted me to have this information. To reject it, to think of my career first, would be to turn my back on God in order to protect myself politically. Gradually, I began to realize that, if God was behind this experience, I had no choice but to embrace it and to trust that God would look out for me. But I couldn't help worrying about how this might change my life.

My integrity was on the line. I couldn't preach these things from the pulpit since that would have been a violation of my ordination vows. Yet, neither could I be a silent witness to what had happened because that would mean abandoning my commitment to God. While I was trying to decide how to proceed, the parade began. People started coming in to talk about odd experiences which had happened to them: one woman told of an appearance by her dead grandmother; another woman described how her deceased husband had materialized at the foot of her bed one night; a third woman stated that the former owner of her house was still living upstairs, although she had been dead for ten years! Other people told of mystical encounters with Jesus, of discovering that they possessed healing skills, of out-of-body experiences during childbirth, of meditations in which they had encountered themselves as they were in a previous life, of feeling that their angels were communicating with them through numbers, music, animals or coincidence. One woman came to relay a message from Jesus, according to her, several years after the loss of our baby in childbirth. She told me that our currently expected child was a boy and that he would be healthy. She was right.

God was drowning me in evidence that something mystical and wonderful was going on in the lives of people around me, something not covered in the confessional statements of the Presbyterian church. It was almost as though God was taking pity on my doubt and giving me so much data to work with that I would have to be blind not to see it. Not only that, but I was learning that there were many people with unusual experiences who were looking for someone to minister to them, people who wanted to know how these events fit into God's plan, who needed support from others who had experienced the same unusual things.

Some of these people organized study groups which I attended. Friends from other religious backgrounds formed similar groups to discuss our various spiritual traditions. That led to the formation of what we called The Oneness Fellowship, a group which eventually included people with Jewish, Muslim, Hindu, Baha'i, Buddhist, Native American and non-religious backgrounds, as well as Christians. We knew that if we talked theology we would spend our time arguing. So, agreeing to discuss only the spiritual traditions of our various faiths, we immediately found a common ground on which to experience our ultimate oneness in God.

It was exciting. The material which we studied—near-death and out-of-body experiences, pre-birth and after-death communication, coincidence as evidence of spiritual guidance, angel intervention, healing, meditation, and other topics including reincarnation—was so popular that I began to teach it to groups in other churches. Then, in July, 1997, I was invited by our synod, a tri-state judicatory of the Presbyterian church, to teach a first-ever course on the subject at their summer school. My presbytery gave me permission to do so.

It was an enormous success, not because I was teaching it but because there were so many people interested in the subject. It was the largest class in the school, filled with enthusiastic people who had their own personal stories to tell and who came to class filled with a powerful sense of God's activity in their lives.

After that positive experience, I began to look for other ways to share the material. About that time, I started corresponding with a classmate of my daughter's by the name of Jill, a young woman with a powerful faith and a burning desire to serve God. She had just discovered *The Messengers,* a book which talks about angel communication, and had learned of the "444 phenomenon."[35] We talked about the various ways in which God was involved in our daily lives, and by January, 1999 we had conceived the idea of co-hosting a website about spirituality. Specifically, we wanted to encourage the church to open up and incorporate some of these phenomena into its belief system.

We launched the site on August 6, 1999, calling it *The Spiritual Bridge* (www.spiritualbridge.com). It included sections on Near-Death and Out-of-Body Experiences, Angels, Pre-Birth and Post-Death Communication, Coincidence and Reincarnation, as well as articles detailing our beliefs and our view of the connection between religion and spirituality. In addition, we included exercises which people could use to examine their personal faith. We began to get responses from around the world, messages such as:

"VERY thought provoking."

"I visited your website and read every word. So great to be able to go somewhere that feels like home."

"My angel communication number is 415. Thanks for letting me know I am not 'crazy'. It's nice to hear that others are sharing the same experiences."

"I often feel spiritually many of the things that you describe, and sometimes I feel very alone in that. I will enjoy keeping in touch with your site."

[*Ominous musical chord!*] But not everyone was pleased with what we were doing. I got a call in January, 2000 from the presbytery functionary who was responsible for my district. He said that they had visited our website and had some concerns. Would I come and talk to the Committee on Ministry about what I was doing? I had no reason to be worried about the summons. I was fully retired, had quit teaching Sunday School, no longer accepted preaching assignments, and the website had nothing to do with them or the church.

I went to the meeting and found myself confronted by eight members of the presbytery. They wore grim faces and telegraphed the kind of righteous displeasure I remembered seeing once when I was sent to the principal's office. As soon as I began to explain why we had launched the site, I realized that this was not a loving discussion among colleagues but a full-blown inquisition. I had been a member of that presbytery longer than anyone in the room, had served as Moderator, had been a member of the Synod Judicial Commission to investigate clergy problems, and had even been elected Clergy of the Year the previous summer. But now I was in big trouble.

Even before I concluded my explanation, it was clear that they had made up their minds. I suggested that, since the site was not connected with the church, it was not within their jurisdiction. They countered by saying that as long as I was ordained they could tell me what I could and could not do. I reminded them that God was not a Presbyterian and that our defense of sectarian creeds probably mattered little to the Almighty. *That* was not the wisest thing I have ever said! The chairman flew into a rage, shouted at me and shattered all pretense that this was a gathering of loving Christian brethren.

I was handed an ultimatum: Shut down the website or give up the ministry. I told them I was not prepared to do either. They called me in for a second session before the Inquisition. The bottom line was: While you're in the ministry, we control every word and action of yours. It doesn't matter that you're inactive. You are a Presbyterian minister and what you say reflects on the whole church. I offered to remove from the site any information which would link me to my former congregation, the presbytery, or the denomination. They thought this was a good idea and I did what they requested. When I went back for approval, they said: Quit the site or quit the ministry. The executive came to talk to me at home, not to discuss my ideas, but to convince me to resign. He hoped that by doing so I would prevent a "bloodbath." I was shocked by his warning, after my forty-three years of ministry.

The committee chair and another administrator from presbytery came to my home to deliver the ultimatum in written form. I was ordered not to preach, teach, conduct the sacraments, solemnize weddings, or do anything that pastors normally do. (I was amused to read, later that summer, the punishment inflicted upon Galileo in 1616: "to abstain altogether from teaching or defending this doctrine and opinion and even from discussing it; and further, if he should not acquiesce, he is to be imprisoned."[36]) If I agreed, I could keep the "Reverend" before my name. I asked if I could conduct funerals. The chair, a friend of thirty or more years, looked me in the eye and said blandly, "John, in order to conduct a funeral, you have to be a Christian!"

When I consulted my family, my children gave me an interesting insight. "You don't agree with what the majority believes any longer. Why do you want to stay in the ministry? We'll tell you why. You want to force them to kick you out, because that will give them a black eye in the public's opinion. You may get satisfaction from that, but it's an unworthy motive."

Wow! Talk about your children becoming your teachers. They were right. So I wrote a letter of resignation and everyone heaved a sigh of relief.

Did the church have the right to demand my resignation? Of course. Within their frame of reference, I was in violation of my ordination vows. But, for me, the whole incident dramatized what I had come to believe, that the church is often more interested in control than in truth. Any larger vision jeopardizes their authority and threatens to upset the theological traditions in which they are invested, and so they fight against it.

Our plea here is for the church to broaden its vision to include more than one point of view. It will be difficult and it will cause conflict, but it is the only path to truth. A marriage in which there is only one partner is barren.

X

MEETING EVELYN

In 1988 I made a trip east to bring our son, David, home from New York City after his sophomore year at New York University. I took along our daughter, Laurie, to keep me company on the eight hour trip. Laurie was married and expecting their first child. The night before the trip, I dreamed about the woman who had been our next door neighbor during all my childhood years. Evelyn has been like a second mother to me and still lives in the same house in New Jersey. I don't remember ever dreaming about her before.

As we were traveling through New Jersey, Laurie noticed that we were going to pass close to my old hometown. She suggested that we stop briefly and see some of the spots which she had visited as a child when her grandparents were still living there. So we drove through town quickly, and I showed her the high school and some other spots of interest—including the homes of some of my former girlfriends—and then we drove down the main street to see the church I attended as a child.

Laurie asked, "Are we going to stop to see Evelyn?" I said, "I'd like to, but we could only stay five minutes, and it wouldn't be fair to drop in unannounced for such a short visit." So, reluctantly, we decided not to stop.

We were already late, but Laurie wanted to see one more place, the spot by the river near the church where she had fed the ducks when she was a child. So we drove to the river and I turned left to cross the bridge. I planned to make a left at the next street and go in alongside the river where the ducks congregated. But I discovered that the town fathers had changed that street to one-way, the wrong way! I said to Laurie, "We'll go down to the next street and come back around the block."

As I started to turn left at the second street, I had to wait for two women who were crossing the intersection. As we drove behind them, I asked Laurie, "Who does that look like?" and she said, "It looks like

Evelyn." And it was! We jumped out of the car and had a wonderful five-minute reunion right there on the sidewalk, a mile from her home.

We had left New Castle, PA eight hours earlier and driven four hundred miles to come to that precise spot in New Jersey at that exact moment to see the person about whom I had dreamed the night before. We could have missed that meeting for any number of reasons: If we had gone to her house, if the first street had not been one-way, if we had stopped on the road one time more or less, if we had arrived thirty seconds sooner or later. Some intelligence had worked out the details perfectly.

Evelyn later told me that they were an hour and a half late taking their walk that day because of her busy schedule.

Chapter 10

SUBJECTS FOR STUDY

We are urging the church, in addition to its study of scripture, to investigate the spiritual material which has been published in the last quarter century, documents which illustrate that we are surrounded by unseen forces which have a direct effect on our lives. Although we cannot deal with these areas of study in detail, we will summarize them here and include a bibliography for those interested in digging deeper.

<u>Coincidence</u>. Coincidence is "God's way of remaining anonymous."[37] I doubt that anyone can hear the story of our meeting with Evelyn without thinking that some remarkable power must have been at work. There are just too many improbable elements surrounding that event. At the very least, we must consider that some unknown law of attraction brings us together in these mysterious ways.

But we must also entertain the possibility that a spiritual consciousness—God, our angel, a spirit guide—engineers these events for reasons we do not yet understand. Our faith tells us that we have an important purpose here on earth. It is logical to assume, therefore, that God has not left us to flounder with no idea of what we are supposed to do or how we are supposed to do it. We are surrounded by heavenly resources which daily guide us along our way. And coincidence is one evidence of that kind of caring oversight.

Many scholars have studied this phenomenon which Dr. Carl Jung termed "synchronicity." Ken Anderson, an authority on the subject, suggests that it represents another dyad. He writes that, since much of our life is cause-and-effect, coincidence is a reminder of the forgotten non-causal side of things. Because there are at least as many unconnected or non-causal events as there are causal ones, a coincidence can be seen as pointing to this missing half of reality. And since that missing half is anchored somehow in the spiritual world, we need to learn more about it if we want to understand the mystery of our existence.

Out-of-Body (OBE) and Near-Death-Experiences (NDE). Raymond Moody's seminal work on NDE's, *Life After Life,* published in 1975, focused popular attention on a phenomenon which had been reported for centuries. It gave us clinical evidence that our spirit is able to exist outside our physical body, and seemed to prove that our consciousness survives death. *Return From Tomorrow* by George Ritchey was one of the earliest accounts of a full-blown NDE, in which the subject saw both the positive and negative sides of the spirit world, what we describe as heaven and hell. More importantly, he had encounters which he was later able to verify, demonstrating to him that the entire experience had not merely taken place in his imagination.

When I first read these books a quarter century ago, I assumed that Christians would rush to embrace them since they seemed to confirm what the church had always taught, that the soul survives physical death. I was wrong. The accounts took place outside of a Christian context and so were unacceptable to many religious authorities. Yet, in the intervening years, we have assembled a massive amount of data which indicate not only that crises can separate body and spirit, but that we can learn how to effect this separation intentionally.

Understanding the significance of the NDE and the OBE can help us develop a larger world view in which we see spirit not merely as a religious concern but as a universal reality. We need to make religion fit that reality rather than trying to distort reality to fit our religion.

Angel Communication. The Bible is filled with angels, messengers who are busy doing God's work. But some in the church believe that the age of angels is past, that they are mythological creatures who no longer fit into a technological world view.

A friend of mine, "Don," has done extensive research in this area. He has a guardian angel he calls "Mark" and with whom he communicates psychically. He once told me how Mark describes their relationship. Mark said that the two of them had "come off the assembly line together," that Mark had been Don's angel in every one of his incarnations. They have an intimate connection which produces learning for both of them. Mark needs to understand something of the human experience, of doubt and fear and lack of faith, while Don needs to be reassured by Mark that he will be given the spiritual resources to complete his earthly tasks. The two of them form a closed energy system. When Don expresses a need or feels a strong emotion, he gives off energy which attracts Mark who is able to capture and preserve that energy within their mutual system. Mark's job is to assist Don in his earthly mission since he has access to much, though not all, of the information which Don needs.

Nick Bunick, whose work is described in the book *The Messengers* by Julia Ingram and G. W. Hardin, was awakened one night and given a mystical message. As he wrote it down, he noted the time he was awakened: 4:44 a.m. In the process of spreading his message, Nick found that more and more people were being awakened at 4:44 for various reasons.

On Nick Bunick's website (http://www.fourfourfour.com) there is a page on which visitors may record their own 444 experiences. There are hundreds of such stories: the three hands of a clock stuck on 4, numbers on the license plate of a passing car, receiving change from a clerk in the amount of $4.44. I read the first two chapters of Nick's book one night before I went to bed. That night I woke up, looked at the bedside clock, and was astonished to see that it was 4:44. Several people I know who have read the book have had the same experience. Jill, my website partner, can attest to being wakened at 4:44 following a dream which had some spiritual significance, or walking through a room, casually looking at a clock and seeing that it "just happened" to be 4:44.

We all have our own guardian spirits. It is important that we learn their language so that we can avail ourselves of their help. How do we recognize their signs? When my daughter was away from her fiancé for a year at school, they had a signal. Something memorable had happened in their relationship at 10:38. So every few days, one of them would dial the other at 10:38 and let the phone ring once. That simple sign let them know that the other person was thinking of them.

Subjective? Absolutely. But that was a specific form of communication. Is Nick Bunick's 4:44 subjective? Again, yes. But if we choose to see it as significant, we can turn it into a channel through which the angels can let us know of their presence. Your signs will differ from those of your neighbor. Jill's "angel number" is 777. Mine is 437.

I need to take a moment here to tell you about my number. I began to recognize it as special when I was a child. I saw it often since it was the house number on the front porch stoop of my aunt's home in New Jersey. As I learned arithmetic, I realized it was a formula: 4+3=7. Later, the number kept turning up, on clocks, on passing trucks, in phone numbers of people close to me, in change from a clerk. Often it appeared at a moment when I was worried about some issue in my life, and I gradually came to see it as a sign of encouragement from my guides. But it was not until I began this book, sixty years after I had first recognized the number as "mine," that a friend came up with some incredible information. He is a math teacher who, though not interested in numerology, is fascinated by numbers. He showed me that my initials, *J.W.S.*, convert to the alphabetic numerals 10-23-19, and that when those numbers are multiplied together, they equal 4370. But that was not all. A short time later, he sent me another shocker. The address of the manse in which we had lived for thirty-one years was *2502 Wilmington Road, New Castle, Pennsylvania.* When those letters are converted into numerals and added together, they equal 437! *And,* as if that weren't enough, when I retired he pointed out to me that I had served 4 churches over a period of…37

years. My life has been bathed in that number! Now, write all of that off to coincidence if you want, but I think it points to something far more significant.

It appears to me that numbers like 111 and 444 are "network" channels to which everyone has access, whereas 437 is my private line. I think everyone has their own private line. In the previous chapter I quoted a comment from a visitor to our website: "My angel communication number is 415. Thanks for letting me know I am not 'crazy'. It's nice to hear that others are sharing the same experiences." The church needs to teach us to be sensitive to these angelic taps on the shoulder, because they tell us that our guides are on duty, eager to help us accomplish our spiritual tasks.

<u>After-Death Communication.</u> For centuries, we have heard stories about the spirits of the dead appearing to the living. Often, we write these tales off as superstition or think of the apparitions as evil. But this phenomenon has an important place in our cultural thinking and has been the basis for some of the most famous works of drama and literature, among them *Hamlet* and *A Christmas Carol* by such diverse writers as Shakespeare and Charles Dickens.

In recent years, this phenomenon has been investigated more thoroughly and is referred to in the research literature as "After Death Communication" (ADC). Bill and Judy Guggenheim, experts on the subject and authors of the book, *Hello from Heaven!*, report that the various types of ADCs which have been noted include: sensing a presence, hearing a voice, feeling a touch, smelling a fragrance, and seeing an image, as well as ADCs that occur during sleep, out-of-body, or over the telephone.

A majority of these events prove not to be grief-induced hallucinations, as many prefer to believe, but actual appearances. We know this is true because of the self-authenticating nature of some of the contacts. In these cases, the spirit gives previously unknown information to the living person which, upon investigation, proves to be true. It is reported that 40% of Americans have had ADCs. Some say that among widows the number rises to over 60%.

Following is a typical example of this type of appearance, which happened to some people I know well.

A good friend of mine died suddenly in February, 1996. Her daughter had a little girl named MacKenzie who was almost two years old, and this child and her grandmother had had a very special loving relationship. MacKenzie was bright and unusually articulate and her grandmother went out of her way to see her almost every day. No one knew how to tell her that her grandmother had died.

Shortly before the funeral service, the mother visited her family to discuss final arrangements. When it came time to leave, she put MacKenzie in her carseat in the rear of the car and started to drive home.

They always talked and sang when they were in the car together, but this evening the child was unusually quiet for a while. Then she started to chatter excitedly, and the mother could tell by her inflections that she was talking to someone. She listened for a while, then asked who she was conversing with. MacKenzie said very plainly, in a somewhat impatient tone, "Grandma." Her mother, startled, asked where Grandma was. Her daughter pointed to the empty space beside her on the seat and said, "Right here, Mommy!"

After a moment the mother asked, "What are you and Grandma talking about?" MacKenzie chattered for a few seconds to the space beside her, then said, "Mommy, Grandma says she's fine now. She's in heaven. And she loves us very much."

When we as religious people decide to study this phenomenon more seriously, we will learn new and significant truths which we can add to the church's traditional teaching about life after death.

Pre-Birth Communication (PBE). While the Near Death Experience explores where we go after death, the Pre-Birth Experience describes where we lived before we were born. There is a growing body of literature which details the reality of life before life, telling of contacts between unborn children and their future parents and of the meticulous care and planning that go into matching incarnating souls with earthly families. Sarah Hinze, in *Coming from the Light,* gives accounts of people who were informed prior to pregnancy about their future children, parents who met their children before they were born, children who vividly recall their life before birth and their journey onto this plane, along with other evidence of the fact that we do not come into existence only at the moment of conception.

This is not a new concept, even though the church argues strenuously against it. Origen, "the most prominent of the church fathers with the possible exception of Augustine,"[38] taught the pre-existence of the soul. Yet, in 553 the Council of Constantinople condemned his ideas. Those who continued to believe in pre-existence and rebirth were persecuted, and this campaign effectively forced the concept underground. Had it not been for this council, the Christian church might well have been teaching pre-existence and rebirth as a basic doctrine all these years.

A friend of mine had an interesting pre-birth experience. She and her husband had two boys but had lost a girl at birth. Attending a women's retreat, she was standing in a crowd of people when she heard a voice. It was so loud that she turned to see if everyone else in the room had heard it also. No one had. The voice said, *You're going to have a daughter, and you are to name her Rebecca. She will be healthy.*

Immediately, she began to argue with the voice. "We don't want any more children, and I don't like the name Rebecca." The voice said, *I will prove it to you.* Later the group shared an exercise in which they were seated at tables identified by the names of women in the Bible. When her name was called, she was told to sit at the table named Rebecca. From that moment on she began to believe.

Despite their efforts to prevent another baby, she became pregnant within two months of this time. She called the baby Rebecca and referred to it as "she" all during her pregnancy. Others close to her worried about this, afraid that it was wishful thinking related to the daughter they had lost. A good friend asked if she would be terribly disappointed if it wasn't a girl. She answered that there was no chance of it being a boy, that she had it on "the highest authority."

When she went into labor, the same problem occurred which had resulted in the death of the previous baby and the doctor had to perform a C-section. Before she saw the baby, she asked the nurse, "Is she all right?" The nurse inquired if she had had an ultra-sound examination. When she said no, the nurse asked how she knew it was a girl. She responded simply, "God told me." The nurse shrugged and laughed it off. Rebecca, now a teen, is a loving child who has been a blessing to her mother.

<u>Reincarnation</u>. We have talked about "life before life" (PBE) as well as "life after life" (NDE). Many church members have no problem with either of these concepts. However, few see the linkage between the two, that life after life may eventually become life before life, that is, life before the next human experience, the next incarnation.

For various reasons, Christian theology does not make room for the concept of reincarnation. This is in spite of biblical texts which suggest it. "Even before the world was made, God had already chosen us to be his through our union with Christ."[39] In answer to Jesus' question as to who people thought he was, the disciples answered, "Some say John the Baptist,…Others say Elijah, while others say Jeremiah or some other prophet."[40] All of these people were dead, indicating that his followers did not think it impossible for the dead to be reborn.

Most Christians believe that we are created at conception and that when we die we become eternal. But, as we have pointed out, eternity cannot be eternal on only one end. If something has a beginning, it must have an end. If we believe that we will live forever, it must follow that we have always existed.

If we have always existed, what have we been up to all this time? We know that our present incarnation is important in our spiritual growth. But how can a single life on earth adequately prepare us to meet the transcendent God? If one incarnation is helpful in our spiritual evolution, why wouldn't two be twice as useful? And what do we do after we achieve heaven, spend eternity in total inactivity? What is it that makes the church resist the idea of multiple human lives when other world religions accept it? The answer is control. If we have an unlimited number of opportunities to "get it right," the church loses its ability to threaten us with hellfire if we do not obey its rules in this current life.

There are a myriad of questions left unanswered by our traditional theology: When do we get to use the wisdom we have accumulated in this life? Why should God punish people eternally for sins committed in the temporal sphere: even we do not punish our children for the next fifty years for a penny stolen in the first grade. What happens to mentally retarded people and those who cannot comprehend the laws of God: if God makes exceptions for them, what other exceptions does God make? How do we account for the vast discrepancies in the lives of people, some living in poverty, some in wealth? At what point does God even out these unfair distinctions? The church needs to reconsider the implications of its belief that we are created in God's image, and open itself to the possibility that we have always existed and will always exist as part of God.

If these glimpses of the world of spirit are true, then organized religion should want to include these subjects within the scope of its study. Why does it recoil from doing so? Because it is afraid of having to rethink its belief system. But these stories are exciting and encouraging, they deepen our faith and fill us with hope. In addition, they reinforce religion's basic message, that God is love and that God's power is a constant reality in our daily life.

XI

THE AMISH

In the area of Pennsylvania where I live, the Amish have a number of long-established communities. We have great respect for their close family connections, their inter-dependence, their hard work and their devotion to their faith. We do, however, grumble about their buggies on the road and the horse manure through which we have to drive. They seem to feel that the modern world has lost its simplicity and thus its connection to God. And they may be right. They believe that living in a centuries-old culture makes it easier to concentrate on the basics of life: family, work and faith.

At the same time, it's possible to look objectively at their lifestyle and see its blind spots. God is not trapped in 1800. To believe that God is available in an antique culture and yet missing from the technological 21st century is to delude ourselves. Spirituality does not depend on using horse-drawn plows rather than gasoline-powered tractors. Kerosene lamps do not necessarily create a more holy aura than electric light bulbs. In the same way that we have been led to discover new technological marvels since the 1800s, God has also led us to new spiritual discoveries.

So we have choices. We are free to live a horse-and-buggy lifestyle in a modern age. Or we can realize that each new age brings advances both on the physical and spiritual sides of life, and that to ignore them is to miss something vital from God's continuing revelation. God is in the midst of life, whether it be the first century, the 1800s or today.

We may smile condescendingly at Amish costumes and lifestyles and think ourselves far advanced by comparison. But consider our religious worldview. It is based on a standard not 200 but 2000 years old! We are convinced, as Christians, that if we revert to the ideas, the theology, the writings and the belief system which developed at the beginning of the Christian era, we will please God and be closer to the truth than those who follow other standards.

Chapter 11

UPDATING THE FAITH

To create our new Christianity, we need only make three changes. We must let go of the following concepts:

- That Christianity is the only true religion;
- That the Bible is the only rule of faith and practice;
- That Jesus is the only Savior of the world.

I can almost hear the hoots and hollers, the cries of astonishment, the shouts of "What does that leave us to believe in?" With that short list, we seem to have taken a high dive off the platform of theory into the pool of total apostasy!

But let's not be afraid to take that plunge. Life is one long swim from the shallow end of life, where we can touch bottom, to the deep end where mature faith can keep us afloat even though we are in over our heads. If we make the journey by degrees, perhaps we will not be so intimidated by the depth of the water at the far end.

To begin with, even though we have always proceeded as though these three articles of faith are true, we see on closer examination that they cannot be literal fact. This will become apparent to everyone some day, perhaps not soon, but in time. True, these doctrines are the traditional pillars of the Christian faith, and they represent fundamental truths that we do not want to lose. But in their literal form they no longer fit the wider vision of the spiritual world which vast numbers of people are coming to accept. They need to be restated. Here is one possible way of doing that. You can undoubtedly come up with even better statements.

- Christianity is a classic belief system which calls us into an intimate relationship with a loving Creator and which contains unique insights into God's plan for human beings.

- The Bible is an ancient and inspired source of God's revelation which contains the teachings of Jesus of Nazareth as well as spiritual wisdom that can guide our faith and practice.

- Jesus is the Way, the Truth, and the Life for Christians, a spiritual master whose message shows us how to join him in the Kingdom of God.

As people begin to redefine the faith along these lines, changes will occur which will allow the church to maximize its potential for good. Let's briefly consider these traditional beliefs.

<u>Christianity is the only true religion.</u> It's amazing, in the 21st century, how many people still believe that this is true. As we have seen, the idea that my religion is the "one true faith" comes from a naive philosophy which puts me at the center of God's concern and places everyone else on the fringes. It ignores the fact that if I had been born in Egypt, for instance, I would now be part of a Muslim group proclaiming "Allah akhbar!"[41]

The belief that Christianity is the only acceptable way to God involves negative attitudes about God, ourselves and others.

First, it assumes that God created a majority of humans knowing that they would spend eternity in hell. It teaches that God condemns them regardless of how faithfully they practice their own religious heritage, how much they seek fellowship with God, and how loving and productive their lives may have been.

Second, it is an admission of our fear. Persons who think differently than we do threaten us. They confront us with the possibility that we might be wrong, so we try to silence them. The most effective way to do that is to convert them, since then they themselves confess that our truth is the superior one. This has nothing to do with openness to God and everything to do with the politics of winning. Such thinking produced the Crusades where Christians held "infidels" at sword point and threatened them with death if they did not convert.

Third, it trivializes God, disparages the experience of our fellow human beings, and turns a deaf ear to what God is trying to tell us through them. God speaks to us all individually. We each receive a different piece of the puzzle of life. We can only complete that puzzle as we join in trying to figure out how those pieces fit together. But the church seems to want us all to have the same puzzle piece. What kind of a silly-looking result is that going to produce?

We need to accept the fact that there are many roads to the divine. Every religion is a different spiritual language. Who would claim that English is better than German? That is a meaningless assertion and anyone who makes such a statement speaks from ignorance and prejudice. Each human language may have its peculiar strengths and weaknesses, but they are all merely methods of communication, different paths to the same destination. The same is true of the various religious traditions. Each is conditioned by its own cultural history and each makes sense within that context. In addition, each brings something valuable to the search for spiritual truth from which we can all learn.

I believe that the new millennium will ultimately bring us to this point of view. It is time to denounce the evil of religious war, to stop killing each other in the name of God. We must outgrow the primitive concept of national gods and sacred soil. Until we understand that God is one, we will not grasp the fact that humanity is one. But when we do, we will stop letting religion divide us from each other and begin to celebrate the fact that we all worship the same God, although we speak to God in a variety of religious languages.

<u>The Bible is the only rule of faith and practice.</u> This is what we have been taught since our Sunday School days, and most of us have never asked the critical questions which would broaden our view.

First, can we really believe that God, who inspired the scriptures through the Holy Spirit, has had nothing to say in the past two thousand years? What about Jesus' promise to lead us into all the truth by telling us *much more* about God's plan for us? Where is that material? If we were to discover it, don't you suppose that we would consider those teachings to be on a par with scripture?

Second, the Bible records an evolving awareness of the character of God and of God's plan for humankind, but it is written from the perspective of the cultural norms of that ancient time. For instance, when it mentions the slaughter of enemies,[42] selling children[43] or punishing them by death,[44] polygamy[45] and slavery,[46] it seems to indicate that these things are approved by God. The people who wrote scripture obviously confused the community standards of their day with the will of God. As a result, there is much in scripture which we can ignore when it comes to literal obedience.

But what else in the Bible is so outdated that future generations will fault us for taking it literally? How about sexism[47] and homophobia?[48] If we can see an evolution of moral awareness in the Bible, why do we believe that the process stopped when the Bible was completed? Increasingly sensitive spiritual minds in the millennia since then have also been touched by the Holy Spirit and have truths to share with us of equal value with what we find in scripture. The process is incomplete, dynamic, ever evolving. If we hope to achieve an intimate relationship with God, it will not be with a God who stopped talking in distant history but with one who engages us in meaningful dialog today.

Third, if we claim that Jesus is God, then his teachings should be uniquely authoritative. But if we look on all of scripture as being equally inspired we place the other writings on a par with the teachings of Jesus, and in a sense we elevate the writers to divinity. At the very least, we claim that they were divinely inspired. Yet they were common men. Thus we affirm that common humans can be inspired by the Spirit to write divine truth. Obviously the same truth holds today and therefore we cannot claim that the day of inspiration ended with the closing of the New Testament canon.

Fourth, while the Bible is true, it is incomplete. There have been tremendous strides in spiritual understanding since the first century. But because the church insists on staying tied to documents which are two thousand years old, it is becoming increasingly irrelevant. No wonder that it is losing credibility. Traditional theology makes as much sense as traditional medicine. Do we think that because we once bled people as a standard treatment, we should do the same today? If a doctor set up a medical practice in our town and based his treatments on medical texts from the time of Jesus, we would be certain to steer clear of him. We no longer use two thousand-year-old theories to guide us in legal or medical matters. To do so would mean refusing to benefit from the world's continuing enlightenment. What makes us think that religion should be any different? If we believe that spiritual concerns ultimately outweigh legal and medical ones, then it should be even more urgent to have the most accurate information about God.

Is a doctor who invents a device to improve healthcare being unfaithful to the medical fraternity? Ironically, some have thought just that. When it became possible to dull a woman's pain in childbirth, some physicians refused to do so because the Bible declared that women were supposed to suffer while giving birth.[49] Hopefully, we now reject that kind of thinking. We need to realize that searching for truth in documents other than the ancient texts is not an act of unfaithfulness to God.

Fifth, in addition to the precepts set forth in scripture, there are basic spiritual laws which govern the universe. Knowledge of these laws not only makes our actions more intentional and their outcome more understandable, but it gives us a whole new insight into scripture. This is because much of what is written in the Bible is based on these spiritual laws, but the laws themselves are taken for granted and never explained clearly. When we understand the particular law, the scriptural application makes more sense.

For instance, in Luke 6:38 we read, "Give to others and God will give to you....The measure you use for others is the one that God will use for you." This sounds to many people to be against human nature, something we have to force ourselves to do in order to gain God's favor. But there is a universal spiritual law of giving which involves the flow of God's abundance. It says that if you are generous with what God has given you, your generosity opens a channel in you which allows God's riches to flow through you. If you do not trust God, if you think you have to hoard things for your own survival, then you plug the very passage which God wants to use in order to bless you. The classic illustration of this is the difference between the Dead Sea and the Sea of Galilee. The former has no outlet, and thus no circulation; water flows in but not out and the result is stagnation. By contrast, there is a constant flow of water through the Sea of Galilee which continually refreshes it and fills it with life. This is the basic principle behind the Golden Rule: What you want to receive, you must give away. Many of Jesus' teachings are based on this law, but the law itself is not spelled out in scripture. Awareness of that law, and many others, gives a new depth of meaning to scripture.

Sixth, modern spiritual accounts help us realize the authenticity of some of the elements in scripture which we have tended to disparage. For instance, the New Testament is filled with angelic activity. However, if you ask many people about the likelihood of angel intervention today, they laugh it off as superstition or say that the age of angels is past. Yet, God's truth is eternal; if a thing was true in Bible times, it is true today. When people are shown the massive evidence that angels are still active, they look at scripture with a new respect. The same thing is true with pre-birth and post-death communication, coincidence, visions and so on. Modern verification of the ancient record is a powerful stimulus to faith.

Jesus is the only savior of mankind. This statement is so important that we will devote an entire chapter to it. But first let us deal with one more pillar of organized religion.

The clergy knows more about spiritual truth than the laity. Although Protestants claim to believe in "the priesthood of all believers," in practical fact we do not take it seriously. This is another distinction between religion and spirituality. Admittedly, the clergy knows more about running a Christian institution than does the average layperson, but we are talking here about the ability to perceive spiritual truth. In that regard, God shows no distinction between clergy and lay.

How does this idea change the way we think? It does away with the hierarchy: we don't need priests to intercede for us with God. That was one of the cornerstones of the first reformation. And that underlines what we have been saying, that we are all plugged directly into the power grid we call God, giving each of us his or her own private line of communication with the divine. But the reverse is also true: God is able to transmit truth directly into individual lives through their unique experiences, so that parts of God's reality can only be accessed in community as we listen to each other's stories.

I had a wonderful example of this some months ago. I was invited to speak to a Sunday School class composed mostly of senior citizens. The pastor had learned of my ouster from the ministry and was anxious for his people to hear my story. I went with some reluctance since it was a conservative church, and I anticipated little support for my point of view. We had a full hour, and I spent the first fifteen minutes outlining the events which had led up to the loss of my ordination. They listened quietly with a kind of formal reserve which I interpreted as lack of sympathy. During the second fifteen minute period, I recounted some of the stories which we have published on our website, explaining that it was events like these which had brought me to my current theological position: stories about dead people appearing to loved ones, angels helping to find lost objects, marvelous coincidences. During this period, I noticed that the attitude of the group began to change: their listening grew more intense and I was connecting in a much deeper way.

Then, astonishingly, I hardly spoke at all during the last half hour. There was a rush on the part of a number of those present to tell their own stories, many of which were revealed for the first time. They didn't want to hear what I had to say. They were eager, almost desperate, to share their personal experiences. I was the first person who had given them permission to do so, simply by telling them that they were not alone.

The witness of laypeople is often more powerful than anything a minister has to say. An inside joke among clergy goes: "A preacher is paid to be good; a layperson is good for nothing." It sounds like an insult when in fact it is a compliment. A heartfelt story from a church member is often more moving than the best prepared sermon.

Whenever I address groups on this material, similar moments of sharing take place. Invariably someone will raise a hand and tell an incident from his or her own life. It always touches me, and it inspires those in the group. This is an example of the priesthood of believers at work, ordinary lay people ministering to each other by relating the activity of God in their lives. It is the old practice of "giving testimony" brought up to date. In this way, people are made aware of the variety of ways in which the Spirit works in our daily routine. The church needs to foster this kind of sharing and give people permission to tell their stories. In doing so, it underline its basic message that God is a practical force in our daily life.

XII

MADISON'S SHADOW

I spent an evening several years ago babysitting our granddaughter, Madison, who was two-and-a-half at the time. At one point, we took a walk around the block. The sun was setting and Madison cast a long shadow. As she ran ahead of me, her shadow kept pace with her. When she stopped to examine it, I told her, "That's your shadow. It goes everywhere you go. See if you can run away from it." So she started running, watching it all the while. I had a moment's regret because I was concerned she would bump into something! But it was fascinating to watch as she discovered and explored her personal shadow.

She raised her arms like a bird, and her shadow mimicked her action. She jumped up and down and her shadow kept perfect time with her movements. She spread her skirt and watched as her two-dimensional twin did the same. Each time, she looked at me with a grin of discovery. It was a kind of magic.

Where did Madison's shadow come from? From the sun. Darkness is created by light! Or, more accurately, by the absence of light. Where there is no light, there is no shadow. The light creates the shadow, but the light can always overcome it. Bring the light close enough and the shadow disappears. Take the light away entirely, and the shadow is gone. I John 1:5 says, "God is light, and there is no darkness at all in him."

Dr. Carl Jung introduced the concept of the "Shadow," the hidden dimension of each personality which contains elements we want to repress. When we deny this part of ourself, we judge certain aspects of our nature to be "bad." This forces us to play a role throughout life, to mask our true self, pretending that our dark side does not exist. Jung stressed the need to embrace the shadow because it contains energy which can enrich and empower our lives and bring us spiritual healing.

Chapter 12

EVIL

Critics of this "heretical" view of God fault it for having a cavalier attitude toward evil—Sin is not real, everything is acceptable to God, evil is merely a false illusion, there is no hell, and so on. In a world where the Holocaust and the World Trade Center attack can take place, how can we believe in a God who is as benevolent and non-judgmental as this book suggests? Don't actions such as these deserve to be punished? How can we create a moral universe if we teach our children that God does not hate evil?

Let me begin by saying that evil is not an illusion. It is exceedingly and painfully real. But there is an illusion. The illusion is that evil can eventually win. If there were any question about this, then God would not be God. So, the discussion must begin with questions about God.

Is God real? Is God in control? Is God perfectly loving? Is God incapable of mistakes? Do we believe that God has a good plan, and that faith means trusting God's plan even when we fail to understand it?

If you say no to any of these questions, then I have no answers for you. But saying yes to them does not mean that we accept the matter of evil unquestioningly. On the contrary, we have to struggle with the problem until we find a working answer to the existence of evil, or our faith will be a hollow exercise that produces no certainty about anything.

That struggle requires us to come up with meaningful personal answers to five questions:

Where does evil come from?

What purpose does evil serve in our lives?

Why do people choose to do evil deeds?

How well do we obey Jesus' commands on the subject of evil?

How can we best combat evil in today's world?

We start from this premise: God is in control of the universe, God's plan for mankind is perfect, and there are no accidents. Therefore, we must look at evil as an inevitable part of that divine plan.

Where does evil come from? The physical universe is a reflection of the spiritual world and thus is filled with divine lessons hidden in plain sight. For instance, everything in nature casts a shadow and those darker shades are often felt to be menacing. In the same way, every positive value in our life automatically creates the potential for its negative opposite to exist, which can be thought of as its shadow. These positive/negative values are created as dyads with their lighter and darker aspects locked back to back. So, love casts the shadow of hatred, hope casts the shadow of despair, good casts the shadow of evil.

Because God is good, however, we discover that the negative shadows cast by those values have no ultimate power to prevail. Psalm 139:12 says, "Even darkness is not dark for you, and the night is as bright as day. Darkness and light are the same to you." What this means is that light and shadow are not opposing forces. In other words, we cannot say that Light is the realm of God while Darkness is a separate power ruled by Satan, and that in the conflict between the two Satan might be the final victor.

There is an eternal difference between light and darkness. Light is a reality. Darkness is the absence of that reality. Light is a positive force. Darkness is not a force or a presence or a quantity of any kind. It appears only when light disappears. Light is not dependent upon darkness, but darkness is totally dependent upon light.

If you enter a darkened room, you can strike a match, illuminate the room and measurably reduce the level of darkness. But the reverse is not true. You cannot bring a quantity of darkness into a lighted room and reduce the level of the light. Darkness cannot win. It can survive only when the light makes way for it. "The light shines in the darkness, and the darkness has never put it out."[50] Darkness exists for a purpose, but it can never overcome the light.

A British woman whose pet dog was killed in the Blitz during World War II wrote this inscription over its grave: "There is not enough darkness in the whole world to put out the light of one small candle."

The "enlightened" person knows that evil is only a shadow, that it cannot ultimately triumph. Yet, we see the results of evil, we feel its hatred, we experience its pain. Because it looks real, we can focus on the shadow instead of the light. And when we choose the darkness and give evil the energy of our belief and our dark deeds, it comes alive, takes form and walks among us.

Why does God permit this to happen? Could not God have created the world incapable of sin? Of course. But that would be a description of heaven. If that was what we wanted, we would never have come into this imperfect creation or chosen to live on the reverse side of the light. Consequently, we would never have achieved the growth we came here seeking. Until we experience the darkness, we will not be able to fully appreciate the light. This brings us to the second question—

EVIL

What purpose does evil serve in our lives? We have come into the physical world precisely because it is here that we are able to experience the shadows. This opportunity is not afforded us in the world of spirit. Only by going through the darkness can we learn to appreciate the true glory of the light. It is illuminating to remember that the most revered saints all experienced what they referred to as "the dark night of the soul." The shadows constantly force us to make choices: Do we face the light of God or the darkness which that light casts in the opposite direction. This is what is meant by conversion, turning from the darkness to the light

One of the most influential books in my life is a tiny volume entitled *Christ In You.* It was published in 1910 in London but does not identify the author, as though it had been dropped from heaven. It contains some remarkable devotional thoughts.

One of its lessons has us think about a kernel of seed corn. When we pick a single kernel from its cob, it is dry, hard, apparently dead. We plant it in the earth as though we were burying it. In the darkness of its grave, two remarkable things happen. First, it comes to life! Secondly, regardless of the position in which we plant it, its shoot turns until it points toward the surface. How does it know how to do this? It is because hidden in the heart of that inert seed is the memory of the sun. That dormant speck of sun inside the seed reaches out toward the great distant sun for reunion, irresistibly drawn back toward the source of its life.

You and I are planted in the darkness of a sinful earth because it is only here that we can experience the distinction between light and darkness. Inside us is a fragment of God, the memory of who we really are, and that internal speck of the divine longs for reunion with God. We have a choice as to how we respond to that longing: do we fill it with God or with something else? St. Augustine understood that there was only one choice: "Thou hast made us for Thyself, so that our hearts are restless until they find their rest in thee." Initially, however, most of us try to satisfy that restlessness with all sorts of things that are less than God—power, sex, money, pleasure, success. And at the moment we choose something other than God, we create the potential for evil.

Why do people choose to do evil deeds? Since we are embodied spirits, divine/human dyads, we possess two radically different natures: soul and ego. These diverse aspects of our self have opposite methods of dealing with reality—love and fear.

The ego, which directs the earthly side of our dual nature, wants to be in charge. It constantly fights God for control of our life. Because it wants to be God, it considers itself separate from God and thus feels alone, exposed, vulnerable. It has no one to depend upon but itself. This fills it with fear and in its fear it tries to defend itself against those whom it perceives to be threats. Thus, fear divides us into frightened and defensive groups and creates an environment which nurtures sin. [Sin is defined here as believing that we are separate from God and therefore from others, and that what we do to other people to defend our ego has no reciprocal effect.]

The soul, on the other hand, knows that God is ultimately in control and therefore it relies entirely on God's love and protection. As a result, it understands that no external danger can harm it and that even death is not a threat. Thus it has no reason to harm others or even to defend itself against violence. Because it sees itself as part of God, it knows that it is one with every other creature and that whatever it does to others, for good or for evil, it does to itself. God's love flowing through it creates a sense of unity with all things, in contrast to the splintering effect of fear..

In the distinction between those two points of view—love/unity and fear/separation—we find the ground on which the conflict between righteousness and evil takes place.

How well do we obey Jesus' commands on the subject of evil? Jesus says some very severe things about the meaning of discipleship. In Luke 6:46 he asks us, "Why do you call me, 'Lord, Lord,' and yet don't do what I tell you?" He warns us of the consequences of disobedience in the Sermon on the Mount: "Not everyone who calls me 'Lord, Lord' will enter the Kingdom of heaven, but only those who do what my Father in heaven wants them to do. When the Judgment Day comes, many will say to me, 'Lord, Lord! In your name we spoke God's message'....Then I will say to them, 'I never knew you. Get away from me, you wicked people!'"[51]

This is scary stuff. How do we know if we're going to be in or out on the last day? We are usually told that "making a decision for Christ," being "born again," is all that's necessary. But Jesus makes it clear that there is a critical difference between calling him Lord and doing what he says. From his own lips we learn that public professions of faith and church membership alone will not get us into the Kingdom. We must live in daily obedience to his commands.

Some of those commands instruct us how to treat evildoers. In Mt. 5:44-45, Jesus says, "Love your enemies and pray for those who persecute you, so that you may become the [children] of your Father in heaven." He goes on to affirm what we have been discussing in this chapter: "For [God] makes his sun to shine on bad and good people alike, and gives rain to those who do good and to those who do evil." Here he tells us that God _loves_ those whom we label evildoers, those we look upon as enemies. Why does God love them? Because they are also God's children, just as we are. Therefore, God blesses them with the same good things that are showered upon the righteous. We are all part of the same family, and we are required to love evildoers simply because they are our spiritual brothers and sisters. When we hate them and try to force them out of the family, we learn, to our consternation, that we exclude _ourselves_ from the family!

Luke 6 enlarges on that command: "Do good to those who hate you, bless those who curse you." "If anyone hits you on one cheek, let him hit the other one too; if someone takes your coat, let him have your shirt as well. Give to everyone who asks you for something, and when someone takes what is yours, do not ask for it back."

Now, I know of few branches of the Christian church which require this kind of behavior as the price of membership. The Quakers come the closest and there are other groups. But the vast majority of Christians ignore this command, calling it impractical, out of date, even dangerous for anyone who attempts to obey it. Precisely! Jesus told us that discipleship is not merely a pleasant social convention but a life of sacrifice, the acceptance of a personal cross.[52] Dietrich Boenhoffer said that when Jesus calls a person to follow him, he bids him come and *die!* This was the original idea behind the practice of baptism by immersion— dying with Christ, being resurrected to a new spiritual quality of life. That's the difference between the Kingdom and the church: the Kingdom requires that we commit ourselves to being change agents; the church too often is committed to preventing change. The Kingdom focuses on redeeming the world; the church focuses on preserving the institution.

The church is ineffective at changing the world because, to a great extent, it has become *like* the world. In order to attract members, it plays down the idea of cross-bearing, it rejects the kind of personal sacrifice to which Jesus summons us. It is more a protector of the status quo than a powerhouse for generating radical world-changing love. But we cannot claim membership in the Kingdom unless we are *different* from the world, unless we have a higher set of priorities, Kingdom priorities. Look at the activities of African American churches during the civil rights movement and you will see the church doing the work that Jesus laid out for it. Discipleship means sacrifice, risking our personal safety in order to bring the Kingdom a little closer. That's what the fellowship of the cross really means. Without that commitment, the church becomes a mere social club.

Why is the church so often reluctant to be an active part of the fellowship of the cross, despite its claims to the contrary? The answer is summarized in one word: Fear. And this fear expresses itself in two ways.

First, our fear-based theology teaches us that God is a righteous God, a punishing God, a God who demands justice. We are comforted by this belief because it tells us that God hates the same things we do and that, when we punish evildoers, we are pleasing God. We forget that it was religious people acting on this very principle who crucified Jesus. When we insist on thinking this way, we prove that we do not understand the meaning of grace. Until we do, nothing will change.

Second, we have watered down the meaning of "conversion" until it means practically nothing. We see it as intellectual assent: when we agree to believe thus and so, the church considers us to be "saved." This viewpoint fails to see that conversion has a behavioral component without which our intellectual statements mean little. If a car runs at the same speed, whether the brakes are on or off, it's safe to conclude that the brakes are not working. If the people inside the church are not markedly different from those who claim no loyalty to Jesus, it's safe to conclude that "conversion" has had little effect on them.

This situation exists because society operates primarily on the basis of a physical worldview motivated by fear and distrust. When we join the church, we often bring with us the prejudices and hostility that we harbored before becoming members. But discipleship to Jesus is supposed to change that focus to a spiritual awareness animated by the love of God. When this does not happen, when we import the world into the church instead of exporting the Kingdom into the world, the church forsakes its fundamental mission.

That is why it is time for a new theology, a modern reformation. We need a discipline that will make the kind of impact on the world that Jesus was calling for. And that means believing Jesus when he tells us that it is love—not violence or retribution or punishment or fear—that will change the world into God's Kingdom

How can we best combat evil in today's world? Today's world is no different from yesterday's world. We can best combat evil by doing what Jesus told us to do, loving others, even if it kills us. Literally. If we don't want to hear that answer, we cannot with integrity call ourselves his disciples. If we go back to the gospels and examine how he lived his life, we have to confess that the choice is non-violence or hypocrisy. What this means, in practical terms, is that we live each day conscious that we are bearers of God's love, that we have volunteered to use the tool of compassion to combat the weapons of fear which others will use against us. We look each day for opportunities to make a difference in the world, to bring the Kingdom just a bit closer, and we do it knowing that love will always outlast hatred, that light cannot be overcome by darkness.

Now, just so you know that I am not totally unrealistic, I am aware that there are times when we have to meet evil with force. It is violence and injustice that have gotten the world into its present condition, and we may be condemned for some time to confront evil with its own weapons. But we must realize that this is only a temporary measure which usually makes matters worse in the long run. We do not defeat evil by acting like those whom we accuse of evil, no matter how we rationalize our behavior. We are to be _in_ the world but not _of_ the world. It is tempting to hate evildoers, but when we do so we are being driven by our ego. If we are Kingdom citizens, we do not fight this battle with earthly weapons. We know that God will bring everything to a just conclusion, and so we can step back and choose to love rather than hate. This is what makes us different from the world and turns us into the blessed peacemakers whom Jesus calls the children of God.[53]

As disciples, our goal is to break the cycle of violence rather than deepening it. Our treatment of prisoners is instructive on this point. Even though we claim that the purpose of prison is rehabilitation, we know that that goal is rarely accomplished. Prison is primarily punitive. It removes people from society for the duration of their sentence. But in many cases, that time is used to harden inmates so that society suffers further pain in the long run. We reap what we sow. If we were committed to breaking the cycle of criminal behavior, we would work with the prison population in a far different way. But we do not make the resources available for that kind of intensive work because it is not a priority for us. Yet, the present system is not working. We need a new approach and there is one available, the old approach which Jesus taught two thousand years ago. If we say that that approach is unrealistic, we imply that Jesus is a fool. In that case, we might as well confess that our religion is a sham. We can no longer tolerate a religion which claims to obey Jesus but does the opposite of what he commands.

Loving our enemies does not mean that we allow terrorism to go unchallenged or that we cease punishing criminals. We are here to build the Kingdom of God on earth, and that means a society in which people accept total responsibility for their behavior. But people cannot care about society until they feel that society cares about them. God has placed us in communities so that we can support each other. These communities—family, church, society, nation, world—are the means by which God touches individuals through other individuals. And in the process we recognize our oneness, our interdependence. We are all cells in a single divine body, and each cell has the power to affect the whole organism, for good or evil. Thus, we need to insure that every other cell is healthy, because a single cancerous cell can eventually destroy the whole body and us along with it.

To achieve this universal health, we have to treat each cell, each person, whether sinner or saint, as an individual. We cannot lump people into groups, view them as lepers and dismiss them. In a moral society we do not dehumanize the evildoer. We recognize that dehumanizing influences have brought him to his present condition and that more of the same will only worsen the problem. We recognize that every soul is worth saving because every soul is our brother or our sister, and within that soul lies a spark of the divine, regardless of how deeply it may be buried. When we confront a destructive act committed through fear and ignorance, we do not respond with fear and its derivatives—anger, hatred, vengeance. The sinner is afraid because his focus is on the physical world; as followers of Jesus, we have a higher vision.

While we hold the evildoer accountable for his actions, we do not deny our own culpability. We recognize the truth of Paul's statement that we reap exactly what we sow.[54] We need to change the structure which allows half the world to suffer from obesity while the other half starves. We need to break the curse of racism which fills succeeding generations with rage. We need to stop putting economic values ahead of human values in dealing with third world nations. By refusing to honor personal human values, we invite the kind of hostility which keeps war happening. It is time to move beyond a pale discipleship that gives mere lip service to Jesus' commands and find a way to make love a practical tool.

I believe absolutely that the world has reached a more spiritual stage of its development than ever before. There is an enormous spiritual revolution sweeping the globe, but because it is so massive it casts an equally large shadow. Governments and the press focus on the shadow since fear sells papers and wins elections. Thus, we hear daily about the events which fall within the shadow, events which make us fear for the future of civilization. But if we were truly motivated by the love of God, we would focus equally on the millions of encouraging and heart-warming stories generated by the light, stories that could give us a totally different picture of the state of humanity and of God's miraculous activity in today's world.

We choose the kind of world in which we live. Jesus said, "Do for others just what you want them to do for you."[55] Do you want to live in a world of light? Then provide light for others. Do you want people to deal with your failings in loving ways? Then love them, regardless of who they are and what they have done. Jesus tricks us into passing judgment on ourselves when he teaches us to ask God to forgive us our sins in the same way that we forgive those who sin against us.

He leaves us to ponder this thought: "Why should God reward you if you love only the people who love you? Even the tax collectors do that!...You must be perfect—just as your Father in heaven is perfect."[56]

XIII

DYLAN'S FAITH

I spent some time recently with my youngest grandchild, Dylan, playing on an enormous construction in a playground near his home. It looked like a castle made of wood, with half a dozen sections joined by wooden walkways, flights of stairs and balconies. Children were running all through the structure, fascinated by the turrets and the windows and all the intriguing crannies to explore.

Dylan was eighteen months old at the time, one of the youngest children there. For a while, he watched the other children playing, then decided to do his own investigating. I followed him closely but made certain not to interfere with whatever he decided to do. He checked once to see that I was behind him and then never again looked back.

Soon he came to a place where there was a difficult turning step through a doorway. He stopped, examined it and then, without looking to check how close I was, raised his hand straight up in the air. It was a clear signal for help. I took his hand and steadied him as he negotiated the step. When he was up, he immediately removed his hand from mine.

I followed him for fifteen minutes or so. Too busy to look back, he was determined to make this journey by himself. It was not something we were doing together, at least in his mind. But on half a dozen occasions, his hand went up, he received the help he asked for, and then he deliberately withdrew his hand again.

I watched with fascination this display of perfect faith. He wanted to conduct his investigation by himself, but there came moments when he knew he needed strength beyond his own. When that happened, he reached out toward a higher power, perfectly confident that it was available to him. But his body language said, Don't do anything for me that I can do for myself!

Chapter 13

JESUS OF NAZARETH

Is Jesus God? Yes…and no.

The concept of a god coming to earth and taking human form is not original with Christianity. Such a being is called an *avatar*, a Sanscrit word meaning "descent." An avatar is a god who manifests in human form in order to bridge the gap between the two worlds and communicate spiritual truth. The human longing for this kind of divine activity is evident in the comment of the little boy who wanted something more than an invisible God to protect him. He said, "I need a God with skin on his face." An eastern mystic once asked, "If God does not come down as a human being, how will human beings love him?"[57]

Most of the world's religions were initiated by the appearance of a teacher whose profound message led his adherents to conclude that he must have come from God. Hindus revere Krishna as divine in the same way that Christians see Jesus as part of the Trinity. But both of these gods in human form were ultimately killed, which raises the question: Can God die? That, of course, is impossible.

To further confuse the question of Jesus' divinity, the gospels reveal the process by which he came to be identified with God. Thomas Sheehan, in his intriguing book, *The First Coming,* lays out this sequence in graphic form.[58] Recalling that the synoptic gospels were written anywhere from two to three generations after the resurrection, he shows that the farther away the biblical writers were from the earthly life of Jesus, the earlier in his life they identified him as divine. Paul (c. AD 50) sees him as Lord at the resurrection; Mark (c. AD 70) speaks of him as Christ at the time of his baptism; Matthew/Luke (c. AD 85) claim that he was Savior at his conception; and John (c. AD 90) sees him as the preexistent Word through whom God made all things.

When we put all of these factors together—the number of avatars in religious history, the myth that God can be killed, the process through which Jesus of Nazareth was gradually transformed into a Christian god—we see how the early Christians took a remarkable Palestinian prophet and elevated him into a being equal with God in order to give authenticity to their new religion.

We do not doubt that God was in Jesus. We do not doubt that he had evolved spiritually far beyond other humans, or that God sent him to be a witness to the truth. All of these are sufficient credentials to warrant our love and discipleship. But we misunderstand him when we interpret his statement, "The Father and I are one,"[59] to mean that he is God. He *was* one with God, but so are we. There is nothing but God, so we are all created of the same divine substance. Jesus' own statements reflect this equality: his comments about us reveal that he thought of us, not as inferiors, but as potential peers.

He says, "Whoever believes in me will do what I do—yes, he will do even greater things."[60] That is a startling prophesy! If he is God, is he telling us that we will be able to outdo God? Elsewhere he proclaims, "God said, 'You are gods.'"[61] This doesn't sound as though he considers us miserable sinners worthy of eternal punishment. He refers to himself as the Light of the World,[62] then calls us by the same term.[63] In addition, he repeatedly refers to himself as "the Son of Man" rather than "the Son of God," as though he prefers to identify himself with us.

So, people see Jesus as both God and man. As with any dyad, these are flip sides of the same reality. One might suppose that the physical (religious/intellectual) side of the dyad would see him as human, and the spiritual side would understand him to be God. Interestingly, just the opposite is true. The church has made him co-equal with God because it is stuck in the belief that the Kingdom has not yet come, that God is distant and judgmental, and that therefore we need a mediator to connect us with God. This is a function beyond mere mortal man, so the church needs to deify Jesus in order to give him the credentials for the task. Confusing the messenger with the message, it has made Jesus *himself* the message.

By contrast, those who have truly heard Jesus' message—*The Kingdom in your midst*—realize that the Gospel message is not about Jesus but about God, about God's nearness and unconditional love. Those who understand that message don't need to turn Jesus into God because they already have God in their midst. So they are content to see Jesus as he saw himself, a prophet, a spiritual master, a mystic who, because he lived in the presence of God, could translate the Kingdom into terms which the common people understood. To force him into the role of divinity is to completely reverse his message.

I believe that we can see Jesus as "lord of life" without thinking of him as "savior of the world." The former, Jesus of Nazareth, has to do with our personal spirituality; the latter, the Christ figure, concerns religious belief.

As we have noted, those who shaped the original Christian religion did not know how to be spiritual without being religious. Therefore they created a new religion to express their relationship with this remarkable man from Nazareth. But in so doing, they kidnapped him, so to speak, and locked him up for safekeeping in their little religious hideaway. That well-intentioned effort was counterproductive, however, since it led in the opposite direction from what Jesus had in mind.

When Jesus said, "I am the way, the truth and the life,"[64] he was not talking about a new religion. He was not saying that we have to become "Christians" in order to understand his way, truth and life. He was talking about a post-religious reality, the revelation that we already live in a spiritual milieu and that God is totally accessible to everyone. That was the crux of his message.

He went on to say in the same passage, "No one comes to the Father but by me." That has always been interpreted to mean that we must be "saved," that only Christians will find themselves in heaven. But Jesus was saying that we come to the Father by means of his way, truth and life.

What is his "way"? It is the post-religious way, the way of total access to a God who is immediately available.

What is his "truth"? It is the revelation that the Kingdom is already here, among us.

What is his "life"? It is life lived in the Kingdom in the presence of God.

Those who think they need a savior expect to find a God who is righteous, judgmental and punishing. But that God does not exist, except within religion. Religion is a key sought by those who have not yet learned that the door to the Kingdom of God has always been unlocked.

We are citizens of our native land by virtue of our birth. We don't have to do anything to earn that status. Even criminals in prison retain their citizenship with all its protections. It is their birthright. By the same token, we are citizens of the Kingdom of heaven by virtue of our creation in the image of God. We don't have to do anything to earn that status. It is our creation-right.

Therefore, we can move beyond the issue of Jesus' divine saviorhood and still retain his powerful relevance for our lives. If he is not God, then he is not the savior of mankind. That removes from us the burden of having to convert the world to our way of thinking, because there is no need for a savior when we properly understand the Kingdom.

Richard Bach, in *Running From Safety,* has an interesting view of this.[65] He asks if there are doctors who treat sick shadows: broken shadows, deformed shadows, missing shadows. He admits that it is a crazy idea, since whatever the body does, its shadow imitates. So it makes more sense to heal the body because then its shadow will also be healed. His point is this: it is just as foolish to treat the body when in fact the body is merely a shadow of the spirit. Whatever our belief leads us to think, our body imitates. This is the psycho-somatic connection. Fixing the body is trying to fix the shadow. What we need to fix is the spirit.

This is precisely what Jesus is talking about when he announces the coming of the Kingdom. In Matt. 4:23ff, it says, "Jesus went all over Galilee, teaching in the synagogues, preaching the Good News about the Kingdom, and healing people who had all kinds of disease and sickness." As soon as he announced the reality of the Kingdom, people started to get well. As their spirits were healed, their physical condition improved. Getting rid of destructive beliefs changed their lives. And the most destructive belief of all was that God is our divine antagonist. Jesus' Good News swept away that false belief. Therefore, we no longer need a savior because God is no longer the enemy.

We understand this in relation to our own children. When we become parents, we do not say to our child, "Now, here are the things you must do in order to earn my love and to avoid punishment for your imperfection." We give them unconditional love, we teach them the highest principles we know, and ultimately we let them go so they can be free to create their own life. We know that they will learn more from personal experience than from all the rules we could ever lay down for them. If they are limited in any way, we help them compensate for their shortcomings. We rejoice in their successes and suffer through their failures. But, basically, our job is to love and nurture them. Can we believe that God, who created this system, does not treat his own children the same way?

We are *not* saying that salvation is unnecessary. After all, Jesus in announcing the Kingdom commanded us to turn away from our sins.[66] But what exactly does conversion mean? The traditional process goes something like this: I am a worthless sinner who deserves damnation. Since Christ was sinless, he does not owe his life to God as punishment. But since he gave his life anyway, his sacrifice can be used to atone for my sin. So I need to accept Christ as my personal savior and petition God to receive me as a sinner redeemed by Christ's death on the cross.

There's a scene from the Disney movie, *Dumbo,* which illustrates this process. When Dumbo finds it hard to believe that he can actually fly, his friend, Timothy Mouse, presents him with a magic black feather plucked from the tail of a crow. Dumbo believes that this talisman gives him the power to fly, and soars into the sky with confidence whenever he holds it in his trunk. But then, as he is ready to fly inside the big top for the first time, the feather slips from his grasp in mid-dive and he panics, thinking he is about to crash. Timothy desperately reveals the ruse, that the feather was just a symbol, and at the last second Dumbo understands, spreads his ears, and flies off into legend.

Dumbo could fly just as well without the feather, but its presence gave him a sense of security. However, it took a literal leap of faith to prove that he did not need magic in order to fly, that it was his birthright. The same thing is true of the man who waited thirty-eight years for healing by the pool of Bethzatha.[67] Ultimately, his prayer was answered but only after he gave up his dependence on some kind of magic outside himself.

If we are acceptable to God after we accept Christ as savior, we are acceptable before we do so, because we do not change God's mind with our earthly rituals. God is not interested in the ceremonies we use but in the earnestness of our desire to be one with God. That's what the Good News is all about: God's immanence, the end of priestly intercession.

The concept of "conversion," of being "born again," is a way of impressing on ourselves that we are physical/spiritual beings and that we have to make a conscious decision to move from a physical to a spiritual consciousness. Jesus requires us to do this; he said, "No one can see the Kingdom of God unless he is born again."[68] But we often fail to recognize that in this passage he does not suggest that we need his assistance to do so. Being born again is a function of the Holy Spirit, a change that takes place when we make ourselves available to the power of God. It has nothing to do with salvation. It involves "conversion," changing our perspective, facing in a new direction. We can do this by simply realizing that we are one with God and opening ourselves to the transforming power of the Spirit. Or we can do it through the practice of religion, seeing Christ as the intermediary. We are perfectly free to do it the religious way until we understand that we no longer need the magic feather.

What is the difference between a personal and an institutional approach to Jesus? His statements to us—"Follow me," "I am the way, truth and life," "You will do greater things than I do"—are all invitations to join in a one-on-one relationship with him, to personally become part of the Kingdom. Salvation is, after all, an individual decision, not a tribal experience. The ancient Jews felt that their salvation came from being part of Israel. We know that our salvation comes from being part of God. It's the difference between a vertical and a horizontal connection, between looking on Jesus as the lord of my life or as the savior of the world. When we see Jesus as our personal spiritual mentor, he becomes an example of how God wants us to think and live. We are then free to share with other people what we have discovered to be meaningful in our own life. When, however, we demand that all others must use our route to God, we move from spirituality into politics. Faith is an individual matter, and ultimately we cannot tell anyone else what he must believe.

This issue is also one of dependency/maturity. When I behave properly because I am afraid of hellfire punishment, I am still acting like a child. People reach maturity when they act justly not because they fear punishment but because they love justice, when they take personal responsibility for raising the moral level of the world. But too many people simply excuse their moral failures. Someone has said, "It is my nature to sin and God's nature to forgive. Nice arrangement!" When I assume that I have a savior whose job it is to forgive anything I do, it takes me off the moral hook. But when I learn that every thought, word and action of mine affects the universe, I am forced to accept responsibility for my behavior rather than trying to squirm out from under it. Forgiveness comes when we have tried our best and failed. But seeking forgiveness when we lack moral discipline is looking for cheap grace; it doesn't fool God and it shouldn't fool us. At bottom, we are all accountable. The idea that a savior exempts us from personal responsibility is a destructive belief.

For many people, religion provides a discipline that they either do not know how, or cannot be bothered, to develop for themselves. Yet, we are charged with working out our own salvation[69] and we are nurtured by God along the way. Dylan, with his year-old wisdom, already knows this. He is determined to be in charge of his own journey. However, he is smart enough to know that there are points where he needs help. He asks for it without embarrassment and expects it to be there. But he also knows that unless he makes a large part of the journey on his own, he will never learn. This is why Jesus said that only those who become like children will enter the Kingdom.

XIV

THE PATTERN

Our daughter, Laurie, is an artist. She has done quite a bit of work with children both in their schools and at the art museum where she was a staff member. The children's classroom teachers became acquainted with her work through these sessions and, as a result, invited her on one occasion to lead an in-service workshop at a private school. She was asked to show classroom teachers how they might teach art projects to their children.

During the workshop, she described a number of projects and tried to stimulate the teachers' own creative juices. But she noticed blank faces in the group and a general lack of comprehension. To illustrate what she was talking about, she took some construction paper and scissors and quickly improvised a puppet, which she assembled with paper fasteners. Although it was not something she had planned to do, she manipulated it for them and added a few offhand comments about how it might be used.

When the workshop concluded, she noticed that several of the teachers showed continued interest in the puppet. One of them picked it up and asked, "Can we take it apart and trace around the pieces?"

The question shocked Laurie. She had created it on the spur of the moment merely as an example of how they could create projects of their own.

She said to the teacher, "I think it would be better if you were to use your own creativity. You could come up with something much better than this."

But the group responded, "Oh, no, we couldn't do anything like that! You're an artist and we're not."

Chapter 14

CHRISTIANITY AS METAPHOR

Christianity is like a two-dimensional paper pattern of the Kingdom of God.

The theme of this book is that we are physical/spiritual beings. We are not our bodies; we are embodied spirits. We are to function on both levels, living in the physical world but not being of the world. We have physical *and* spiritual senses, and the goal of our religious practice is to allow our spiritual senses to guide our physical behavior. Living a life which straddles and balances both sides of our nature is extremely difficult, and yet that is precisely our goal as spiritual people.

Every aspect of our life can be divided into two different elements which correspond to these two sides of our being, the soul within the body. Examples of this double relationship are everywhere.

• The intact peanut shell is not the edible part of the plant; its nourishment is not available until the shell is cracked open.

• Tele-*vision* does not refer to the piece of furniture sitting in my living room. That is merely the physical object through which the programming is transmitted. Therefore, if I sit and stare at an unplugged set, I miss the essential experience. When it is turned on, the set reveals its inner mystery and the magical vision becomes a reality.

• The word *church* calls to mind a building with a spire. Yet the word existed long before the development of church buildings. It comes from the Greek word for "lord" and refers to a body of people who worship Jesus as Lord. The child's hand trick—"This is the church, This is the steeple, Open the doors and see all the people"—is a graphic description of this truth. A building cannot become a church until it has a worshipping community inside. But that community is usually invisible to the casual passerby.

• A paper puppet, snipped out impulsively in frustration, is not meant to be a permanent work of art. It is a symbol of the creative process. When we do not understand the process, we treat the bits of paper as icons. But possessing someone else's discarded efforts does not necessarily make us more creative.

Since God is spirit and we are flesh, God's message must be dressed in human terms or we would not be able to comprehend it. But we have a bad habit of confusing the vehicle with the message. We tend to focus on the mechanism through which the message is communicated, rather than looking beyond that mechanism to the message itself. We look at the shell instead of cracking it open to get at the nut.

The written word in scripture is a physical vehicle through which the truth of God is transmitted. The words themselves are not the truth, because no human words are capable of containing the whole truth of God. To make that truth understandable, to scale it down so that it will fit inside our little words, we must simplify it and shape it to match images with which we're familiar. But then we tend to worship those words as though they were the literal and final truth.

When we look at scripture, particularly the parables, we are seeing the physical outer story, not the inner spiritual meaning. Jesus used parables precisely because they functioned on two levels. When we read them, we have a choice: we can listen to the cover story, or we can dig deeper and hunt for the metaphorical truth. No thinking person believes that Jesus' stories are really about horticulture or baking or real estate or investments or fishing.[70] The parables are metaphors. Although the surface story concerns all these subjects, they are actually visible pointers to an invisible and more subtle reality.

Jesus told cryptic stories in order to fulfill the promise in Psalm 78: "I will use parables when I speak to them; I will tell them things unknown since the creation of the world."[71] Since seeds, weeds, yeast, pearls and fish *have* been known since the creation of the world, he must have been referring to something else. All of these parables concern the Kingdom of God, and each of these items represents something else. Jesus never says "The Kingdom of heaven is." In every case he says "The Kingdom of heaven is *like this*." Why? Because the Kingdom of heaven cannot be described in human terms. It can only be experienced. So, the Kingdom is *like* a valuable pearl. How is it like a pearl? He doesn't say. We have to figure that out for ourselves. The Kingdom is *like* yeast. How? He leaves us to answer our own question.

He does say something quite disturbing, however. Asked in Mark 4 why he used parables, he quoted from Isaiah: So that "They may look and look, yet not see; they may listen and listen, yet not understand. For if they did, they would turn to God, and he would forgive them." This passage sounds as though Jesus didn't want his hearers to understand what he was saying. That's nonsense, of course. So it must mean something else. It's like the difference between doing your own math problems in school or sneaking a look at the answers in the back of the teacher's book. Copying them down can get you an "A", but it won't make you any smarter. Jesus didn't try to explain the Kingdom because the answer to the question, "What is the Kingdom?" is not intellectual, it is experiential. It's like the old saying about the horse and the water. You can't drink for the horse; it has to drink for itself. Even Jesus cannot experience the Kingdom for us. Each of us has to do it for himself. If we don't struggle with it personally, we get no benefit from it.

Now, perhaps, we can go one step farther and say that much of scripture is also metaphorical, not just the parables. The Bible is not *the* truth, it merely points us toward the truth. The church has always rejected this view. It has a vested interest in interpreting the Bible literally, because its authority is tied up with the Bible's *outer* story. It can control words printed on pages, but it can't control the interpretation of those words by the people who read them. Nevertheless, it tries to dictate what those interpretations should be. That's why the presbytery told me that my vision of a former life was unacceptable. The church sees the outer story and the inner meaning of scripture as one and the same. This is the meaning of "literal interpretation." But the inner meaning of scripture is spiritual and cannot be arbitrarily dictated by any religious authority.

So, biblical teachings are merely the intact peanut shell, the silent television set, the empty cathedral—a package for the truth. But we have been taught from childhood that the package itself is the message. Most of us have gone through the same classic routines, learning Bible stories, memorizing scripture verses, attending Sunday School and worship, using proper religious terminology. All of this is merely tracing around someone else's pattern. It does not make us spiritual any more than copying an artist's creation makes us artistic.

The package is not the message. The message is inside and no one can open that package for us. We have to seek the inner truth for ourselves. When we do, we enter the dimension of experience: we taste the nut on our tongue, we are moved by the emotional power of the television program, we feel the joy of a loving community, we experience communion with God.

Mark 4:33-34 reports that Jesus told the people as much as they could understand. He used only parables, "but when he was alone with his disciples, he would explain everything to them." Wouldn't we love to know what he told them! But this "secret" teaching about the Kingdom was not written down. Some feel cheated when they realize that the most important part of Jesus' teaching is missing from scripture. *But this is the whole point!* The deepest truth is not found in scripture. It is not an idea to be taught but a reality to be experienced. It is only revealed to those who choose to become disciples of Jesus. That does not mean merely church membership. It means seeking personal communion with him, it means meditating and listening to him speak, it means searching for the "much more" that he wants to tell us through the inspiration of the Spirit, it means wrestling with scripture until we get beneath the printed words and hear the voice of God. It is like the difference between receiving a letter from your lover and holding his or her hand.

Now, the foregoing prepares us for the final insight. Christianity itself consists of a classic outer story which encloses the inner truth of the Kingdom. That outer story is not literally true, however, any more than the story of the Good Samaritan pretends to describe a real event. It is another metaphor, a way of dramatizing the need to turn from darkness to light. But because we have been taught to take that outer story literally, we act out our belief that the door to the Kingdom can only be found inside the church. True discipleship, however, is a far different thing.

It is significant that Jesus revealed these inner truths only to his disciples. Who are his disciples? Certainly Judas did not understand the Kingdom, but it is clear that Paul did. So it had nothing to do with being one of the twelve. Paul became a disciple even though he never met Jesus in the flesh. It is equally possible for us to do so.

But discipleship is different from church membership. We recognize the truth of the old spiritual that says, "Everybody talkin' 'bout heaven ain't goin' there!" It takes something more, what Jesus refers to as being "born again," or "born from above" as an alternate translation of John 3:3 goes. Jesus makes this clear in John 3:6: "A person is born physically of human parents, but he is born spiritually of the Spirit." He is affirming what we have said repeatedly, that we are physical/spiritual beings. Our parents helped create our physical body but they did not create the soul that inhabits that body. That soul has always belonged to God. In the same way that we are born into the world through our connection to our mother, we are reborn into the spiritual world by our connection to God. And as we had to cut the umbilical cord to become physically separate from our mother, we have to cut the cord of tradition that ties us to Mother Church in order to know the freedom of true spirituality.

Therefore, we need to study the teachings of Jesus to see how they can be reinterpreted in a way which is more consistent with what we know of God. The traditions which sprang up around his life and teachings are one way of looking at these things, a way heavily slanted toward the thought patterns of a world two thousand years gone. Those teachings are just as meaningful today, but the context in which we have received them is badly out of date.

Just one example will suffice here. The heart and core of the faith is the resurrection. But this part of our belief system needs to be reexamined. In the first place, a physically resurrected Jesus would mean that he ascended in his human body to heaven. This of course is preposterous. Heaven is not a physical place. It is no more possible for a human body to exist there than it is for me to walk through my television screen and participate in the movie I am watching. For another thing,

Jesus' "resurrection" body was spiritual—it appeared and disappeared, entered locked rooms, was unrecognizable to close friends. In addition, the concept of his rising from the dead suggests that physical life is supreme, preferable to spiritual existence, and that death needs to be overcome. All of this reflects Judaism's poorly developed eschatology and ignores the fact that we are already an eternal part of God.

The tomb is the outer story. The living Jesus is the heavenly truth which emerges from it. The cross did not destroy Jesus. Physical death is not the end of life. That is the message of the gospel. Focusing on a story about a reanimated body distracts us from that message and makes a religious rather than a spiritual point. The fact is that the Jews thought concretely rather than mystically. Thus, when they saw Jesus alive, they assumed that his body was a physical one. The gospel record is confused and misleading on this point. In the Emmaus road incident, Luke tells us that Jesus was at first unrecognizable and that later he disappeared.[72] Clearly these are not the attributes of a physical body. Yet, further on in the same chapter, Jesus invites the disciples to touch him, assuring them that he is not a ghost.[73] So the record supports both those who claim that his resurrection body was spiritual and those who say it was physical. The only way we can have it both ways is to see it as another dyad.

Jesus promised, "Because I live, you will live also."[74] If we look at the resurrection from the point of view we have been discussing throughout this study, he seems to be saying, "We are all part of God and therefore we are eternal spirits; when this life is ended and death is past, we will live with God." If the bodily resurrection is the whole point of the story, it sends a message that we are totally unlike Jesus since you and I will never be raised physically from the dead. But he was saying just the opposite, that we *are* like him, that we will be alive after our death, that he goes before us, and that he is preparing a place for us.

Easter is the promise of eternal life, not because we joined a religion which hadn't even been invented yet, but because we are like Jesus, created in God's image, part of eternity. That is the really Good News, despite the church's attempt to turn it into one more religious dogma.

This is only one example of how we need to rethink the traditional doctrines in scripture. We are not saying that those doctrines are unimportant. It is valuable to learn them as children because they form the grammar of our religious mother tongue. But there comes a time when we need to throw away the paper patterns we inherited from others and start to create our own.

When Jesus tells us that we will "do even greater things" than he did, we are tempted to say, "Oh, no, we could never outdo you. You're holy and we're not." But trusting our own intuitive wisdom and discovering our own spiritual truth is the only path to mastery.

XV

THE GOLDEN BUDDHA

Jack Canfield tells the story, in *Chicken Soup for the Soul,* about visiting Thailand in the fall of 1988 with his wife, Georgia. In Bangkok, they toured the city's Buddhist temples. One place, called the Temple of the Golden Buddha, left an indelible impression. It is very small but is dominated by a ten-foot tall, solid-gold Buddha. The statue weighs over two-and-a-half tons and is valued at almost two hundred million dollars!

Curious, they looked into the history of this marvelous work of art. They discovered that, back in 1957, a group of monks planned to relocate a large clay Buddha from their temple to a new location. When the crane tried to lift the giant statue, its weight was so great that it began to crack. The head monk, concerned that they might damage the sacred Buddha, and to protect it from the rain, had the statue lowered to the ground and covered with a canvas tarp.

Later, checking on the Buddha to see if it was staying dry, he shined his flashlight under the tarp. The beam picked up a bright glint under the statue's clay surface. Fetching a chisel and hammer, he began to chip away at the clay and saw the gleam grow brighter. After many hours of labor, the monk stood face to face with the extraordinary solid-gold Buddha.

The full story began two hundred years earlier. At that time, the Burmese army was about to invade Thailand which was then called Siam. The monks, afraid that their precious golden Buddha would be looted, covered it with a coat of clay. Unfortunately, the Burmese soldiers slaughtered all the monks, so the secret of the golden Buddha remained intact until the statue reemerged in 1957.

Chapter 15

LIVING IN THE KINGDOM

Jesus' message about the Kingdom of God is like the Golden Buddha. For centuries, it has been obscured by muddy layers of church politics. The clay veneer that forms the religious institution has shrouded it so completely that the dull surface is all that most people see. But some have glimpsed the gold hidden beneath the surface and have become disillusioned by the cracked exterior. The task of this and future generations is to expose the extraordinary beauty that lies within.

Having dealt with the church hierarchy as a pastor for over forty years, I realize that the establishment is not going to passively move over and make room for this alternate point of view. But this movement needs to remain inside the church if that is at all possible. Why? Because we all share a common loyalty to Jesus of Nazareth. Christianity is my religious mother tongue. I may have a different accent than my brothers and sisters in the mainline church, but we all speak essentially the same language. We need to test our ideas by dialoging with one another, with the goal of enriching our mutual journey.

Deciding to share our witness inside the church is the most difficult of the three options open to us.

1. We could go along with the majority and abandon the struggle for change.

2. We could leave the church and write it off as hopeless. Or

3. We can stay engaged and try to share our ideas with those in the church.

Some members will respond positively to what we have to say, but we will have to deal with the hostility of those who think of us as heretics. Instead of becoming discouraged by this reaction, we need to see it as a law of nature. We began this book by quoting Newton's first law of motion, that an object (or institution) continues in the same direction until some unbalanced force is applied to it. The church probably feels that the heretics who are currently pushing for change are that "unbalanced" force, in more ways than one! Now, we end the book by quoting Newton's final law of motion: "Every action has an equal and opposite reaction." When we push the church, the church can be expected to push back.

I worship regularly with the local congregation where I spent a year as interim pastor. Most of the members are cordial and supportive, but a few keep their distance for fear of contracting spiritual leprosy. I can't blame them. They've never had a defrocked preacher sitting in their midst before! I go because I love the people and because I need the fellowship. From their number, several people have come forward with a desire to form study groups. In these groups, which meet in homes during the week, we are free to discuss new ideas without fear or interference. As the group members strengthen their beliefs, they become less self-conscious about sharing them with others. Although it is not our intention to try to "convert" anyone, we are on the lookout for those who are searching for something beyond the traditional theological viewpoint, hoping that they will eventually find their way into our groups.

Confining our efforts to small gatherings which meet at times other than Sunday morning, we are able to maintain a balance between large corporate worship services and small discovery groups. Formal morning worship does not allow for wrestling with new ideas, sharing stories and ideas, and challenging each other. In the same way that the early Jewish Christians attended both synagogue services on Saturday and Christian worship on Sunday, we must try to balance the two elements in our belief system, the traditional and the innovative. We cannot urge others to be sympathetic to our point of view if we lose touch with the religious culture from which it sprang. The church gives us roots while the group gives us wings.

If we disconnect from the church, we become just one more cult within an already splintered establishment. One thing that can kill this reformation is any attempt to organize it. Unless it remains spontaneous, it too will eventually shut out the voice of the Holy Spirit. Therefore, each group will have its own style, agenda and, perhaps, even its own beliefs. This lack of order will seem chaotic to many who feel comfortable only within a tightly regulated system. Some structure is inevitable, but it must never be seen as final. We are on a journey to the Kingdom of God and we cannot pitch our tents until we reach our destination. The trouble with the church is that it settled down long ago in the wilderness and refuses to budge. We must be different.

What are the marks that distinguish this movement from mainline Christian practice? This is a very subtle thing, because we do not want to appear judgmental or elitist in our description. Many churches already embrace part or all of the elements which we think are important. But there are two main differences between those interested in spiritual renewal and those who hold standard religious beliefs. The first is the desire to remain open to any new word from the Lord, as opposed to the usual church agenda—telling again the old, old story that we have loved so long. The second is the conviction that God accepts us completely as we are, in contrast to what we usually hear from the pulpit, that we are sinners who need to be rescued from divine punishment.

Let's mention some of the personal lifestyle characteristics which distinguish those searching for a new spirituality.

Prayer. One is certainly prayer. But we pray with a slightly different frame of reference from many in the church. Since we are part of God, we do not feel the need to beg for things that God is reluctant to give us. We understand that all of God's resources are available to us and that our faith in their availability is one of the factors that makes it possible for us to receive them. As a result, we thank God for what we need, knowing that God answers our requests even before we make them. We take literally the promise of Jesus in Matt. 21:22, "If you believe, you will receive whatever you ask for in prayer."

Being aware that we are part of God makes us conscious of God's presence in our life at every moment. So, rather than "saying our prayers" at designated moments, prayer for us is a constant sense of being in the Presence, of conversing throughout the day, of asking for help and giving thanks. We live in the moment, paying attention to every evidence of divine protection, guidance and blessing. These may involve any number of things: numerals which are used by angels to get our attention, coincidences which turn out to be divine guidance, ideas which pop into our minds at just the right moment to answer a question, or unexpected opportunities to help someone. We may record these experiences in a journal or share them with our group.

Meditation. We also meditate. Meditation is the other side of the prayer cycle. If prayer involves speaking to God, meditation is listening to God. We need constantly to refresh our link to God. Meditating daily is a way to slow ourselves down, to cut through the tension of the day and get a fresh perspective on God's priorities for our lives. We ask questions in our meditation, listen carefully for answers, and record them in our journal. We seek a deepening inner peace which we can carry with us when we are not actively meditating. Most of all, we remind ourselves that we are not our body, that our primary duty is to communicate God's light and peace to those around us, and that the tensions of the day are the result of investing too much in our ego. So we step back spiritually and remember that we belong to God and not the earth, and that some day we will laugh about the problems which seem so vexing when we lose perspective.

Angel Communication. We live in close touch with our angels. We talk to them, call them by name, put them to work, thank them for their assistance, and share stories about how they have helped us. We are familiar with *The Messengers* which talks at length about the 444 phenomenon by which our angels make their presence known. We also know that 111 and 1111 are numbers which indicate special moments of connection with angelic beings. As I was writing this section, someone e-mailed me the address of a website on angel communication using numbers, particularly 444 and 1111.[75] We have a page on our site that deals with this type of story, and the writer thought we might be interested in the other site. I looked it up and spent some time reading accounts from people who had experienced the same kind of angelic phenomenon that we had. It is reassuring, when you begin to doubt your own perceptions, to have someone else say, in effect, "You're not crazy. That sort of thing happens to me all the time."

To make the story even better, while I was still working on this section of the book, a friend whom I had not seen for several years called. She had no idea about our website, about this book, or about my connection with angel numerology. All she knew was that I might be open to mystical things. She said, "I've been having this strange experience for months, and it occurs five or six times a week! It's like someone is trying to communicate with me, but I don't understand what they're trying to say. It seems that every time I look at the clock, it says 11:11." I roared in amazement. She had never heard of this phenomenon and assumed it was only happening to her. The timing of her call was a gift to me, confirmation from my angels that this technique is a legitimate means of heavenly communication.

Among their many other skills, angels are good at helping us find lost articles. Following are two typical examples. A friend of mine, Linda, asked her angel, whom she calls Gina, to help her find a valuable diamond heart necklace. Her husband had given her the necklace, but he frequently commented about how careless she was with her jewelry. When she discovered that she had mislaid the necklace, she searched for it for days, unwilling to admit to her husband that she had lost it. She convinced herself that he had hidden it to teach her a lesson. Finally, she decided to end her torture and admit her carelessness so that he would return the necklace. He responded by saying, "Well, I guess that's the last piece of jewelry I buy for you!" She stomped off to her room, climbed into bed and cried out in a silent, angry voice, "Gina, if my necklace is in this house, will you *please* show me where it is!" Immediately, she got up and walked around to her husband's side of the bed. In her mind, she saw a scene: it was several weeks earlier and she was standing in that same spot. She had taken off the necklace but, instead of putting it away, had laid it on the bed on top of the comforter. She touched that spot. She could then see a hand pulling down the comforter so someone could get into the bed. She realized that anything on the bed would have fallen to the floor when the comforter was pulled down. She got down on her knees and immediately saw the necklace on the floor between the bed frame and a cedar chest. Gina had heard her plea and in less than fifteen seconds had responded.

Jill, my website partner, has a similar story. Her husband, Richard, lost his cell phone. He had been moving things from a storage locker that day and had had the phone in his coat pocket. He looked everywhere. He tried calling it and walking around the house to see if he could hear it ring. He thought he might have dropped it while walking their dogs, so he and Jill went to the park late at night to try to locate it. Finally they returned home and searched the house again. In exasperation Jill asked her angel, known to her as George, to show her the cell phone. Shortly afterward, she went to the basement where Richard was watching TV. Although she usually sat beside him on a loveseat, she went to another area of the basement to a chair she almost never uses. From that position, her view of the TV was obscured by a folding screen used to hide their treadmill. She sat there for about fifteen minutes, reading. Finally, Richard got up and said, "Let me move that screen so you can see the TV." He folded the screen, leaned it against the wall and went upstairs. When Jill got up to leave, she saw the cell phone lying on the floor. It had been under the screen. She asked Richard if he'd been in the basement that day, and he told her he'd been there only once. The oddest part of the story, Jill adds, was that she had been reading an article about the demise of John F. Kennedy Jr.'s magazine...*George!*

Dreams. We also pay close attention to our dreams. Dreaming, which John Sanford calls "God's forgotten language," is a channel through which God can reflect to us what is happening in our lives.

Have you ever wondered why we are unconscious for a full one-third of our lives? God could have made us so we didn't need sleep. The reason that we spend so much time in an altered state of consciousness is, I believe, so that we can renew both body *and* soul. Since we are eternal beings, our connection to the spiritual world is much stronger and more significant than we think. We have come here with an important spiritual task to accomplish, and we cannot complete it without being constantly in touch with headquarters. Part of being physical involves losing the memory of our true spiritual identity. We compensate for this by entering an alternate state each night in which the conscious mind barriers dissolve and we are open to God's instruction. I personally believe that we are active spiritually while we are asleep, studying, learning, having our goals reinforced, honing our spiritual skills. Dreams may well be the fractured memories of these nighttime adventures, seemingly bizarre because our conscious mind does not have the tools to understand their origin.

We believe that dream interpretation is a valuable way to understand what we are feeling, what kind of progress we are making, and what choices God is presenting to us. As a result, we teach ourselves to remember our dreams, we write them in our journals, meditate on them, make notes about what they mean, and share them with members of the group who often help us interpret them.

Reading. Reading is a priority with members of our groups. Most of us are voracious readers. We read everything in the field of spirituality that we can get our hands on. It is dangerous and expensive to turn us loose in the Spirituality or New Age sections of a book store! We are hungry for new insights into the spiritual world, anxious to read about the experiences of others that challenge us and stretch our thinking.

We also read material from other religious traditions to see what insights they can offer us, since we believe that every one contains part of the truth. In this regard, an image came to me once when I visited a lumber yard. There I saw an unbroken pallet of plywood on the side of which was painted the company logo. I realized that if I bought one of the sheets, I would only be able to see a narrow sliver of that design, a ribbon of color that would make no sense by itself. It was a reminder that each religion has its own slice of God's truth and that we have to put them all together in order to get the whole picture.

These ideas are not threatening, as they seem to be for many church members. Rather, we are able to sift through the various ideas presented, integrate concepts that harmonize with our own worldviews and discard those that do not. This requires the ability to be open without being gullible. New stories, ideas and experiences are mined like jewels and brought to group meetings to be shared and relished by the members.

Moral Accountability. I mentioned earlier that one of the things that distinguishes us from more traditional Christians is "the conviction that God accepts us completely as we are, in contrast to what we usually hear from the pulpit, that we are sinners who need to be rescued from divine punishment." This is taken by some to suggest that we don't believe in sin and that God automatically forgives everything we do. Nothing could be less accurate. In fact, this worldview increases our sense of moral accountability We believe that every word, action and thought has energy, and that energy never dies. As a result, everything we do keeps on having its effect on the universe and we are responsible for that effect. In addition, since we share God's eternal existence, we have had many lives prior to this one. Part of a belief in reincarnation is the concept of karma which teaches us that we reap what we sow, that, in the words of Jesus, the measure we give is the measure we receive.[76] We know that the smallest detail will be part of our permanent record and that we are totally answerable to God. I believe that this worldview has enormous potential for making the world a more moral place.

Discipleship to Jesus. Most important, we are disciples of Jesus of Nazareth. As we said earlier, we can view him as lord of life without having to think of him as savior of the world. This involves personal communion with him through meditation, it means searching for the "much more" that he is anxious to tell us, it entails letting his teachings guide us and his presence accompany us in our daily routine. Some who have had near-death experiences have encountered a "being of light" whom they identified as Jesus. So we understand that he is speaking literally when he refers to himself as "the light of the world." We know that he has a major place in God's plan for us, and thus we embrace him as master, teacher and friend. He is the face we put on God, our model for life, the image of what God's spirit can help us become.

Spiritual Perspective. Finally, our worldview tells us that we are spiritual actors dressed in costumes of flesh playing out a divine drama on an earthly stage, writing the script as we go. God is the sole member of the audience, the angels are the prompters, and our worst antagonist on stage is our best friend off stage. Because we are developing the plot as the play proceeds, what we are doing is tremendously creative. It has the power to turn a tragic first act into a triumphant conclusion which will have everyone on their feet cheering through tears of joy.

When we view our life as a spiritual drama, we can relax and enjoy the experience, with its comedy and its tragedy, knowing that when the curtain comes down we will all walk backstage, take off our makeup, compliment each other on our performances, and critique how we might play our parts more convincingly in the next production.

* * * * * * * * * * * * * * * *

So, we have reached the end of our little excursion into heresy. Let's conclude with one of Ben Franklin's comments about religion. He said it is like a man traveling in foggy weather. He looks around at the people walking along the road with him. Those at some distance from him are wrapped up in the fog and barely visible. But near him everything appears clear, although in fact he is as much in the fog as any of them.

Even when the fog is thickest, we can see far enough to take the next step, and if we stay on the road it will eventually lead us home. Since we all have the same destination, common sense tells us that it will be much more profitable, and enjoyable, to make the journey together.

Suggested Reading List

After Death Communication

Hello From Heaven: A new field of research confirms that life and love are eternal, Bill Guggenheim and Judy Guggenheim. Bantam Books, New York, 1995.

Reunions: Visionary Encounters with Departed Loved Ones, Raymond Moody, M.D. Ballantine Books, New York, 1993.

Talking to Heaven: A Medium's Message of Life After Death, James Van Praagh. Signet, New York, 1997.

Angels

Angels Among Us, Compiled by the editors of Guideposts, Carmel, NY, 1993.

Book of Angels, A, Sophy Burnham. Ballantine Books, New York, 1990.

Brush of An Angel's Wing, Charlie W. Shedd. Guideposts, Carmel, NY, 1994.

Messengers, The, Julia Ingram and G. W. Hardin. Pocket Star Books, New York, 1996.

Rustle of Angels, A, Marilynn Carlson Webber and William D. Webber. Guideposts, Carmel, NY, 1994.

Coincidence

Coincidences: Chance or Fate?, Ken Anderson. Blandford, London, 1991.

Small Miracles: Extraordinary Coincidences from Everyday Life, Yitta Halberstam and Judith Leventhal. Adams Media Corp., Holbrook, MA, 1997.

Small Miracles II: Heartwarming Gifts of Extraordinary Coincidences, Yitta Halberstam and Judith Leventhal. Adams Media Corp., Holbrook, MA, 1998.

There Are No Accidents: Synchronicity and the Stories of Our Lives, Robert H. Hopcke. Penguin Putnam, New York, 1997.

Dreams

Dreams and the Search for Meaning, Peter O'Connor. Paulist Press, New York, 1986.

Dreams: God's Forgotten Language, John A. Sanford. Crossroad, New York, 1986.

Dreams: True Stories of Remarkable Encounters With God, Ann Spangler. Zondervan, Grand Rapids, MI, 1997.

A HANDBOOK FOR HERETICS

Modern Theology

First Coming, The: How the Kingdom of God Became Christianity,
Thomas Sheehan. Random House, New York, 1986.

*Christian Conspiracy, The: How the Teachings of Christ Have Been
Altered by Christians,* L. David Moore. Pendulum Plus Press, Atlanta,
1994.

*Why Christianity Must Change or Die: A Bishop Speaks to Believers in
Exile,* John Shelby Spong. HarperCollins, New York, 1998.

Near-Death Experiences

*Closer to the Light: Learning from the Near-Death Experiences of
Children,* Melvin Morse, M.D. Ballantine Books, New York, 1990.

*Heading Toward Omega: In Search of the Meaning of the Near-Death
Experience,* Kenneth Ring. William Morrow, New York, 1984.

Life After Life, Raymond A. Moody, Jr., M.D. Bantam Books, New York,
1975.

Return From Tomorrow, George G. Ritchie, M.D. Fleming H. Revell Co.,
Tarrytown, NY, 1987.

Saved By The Light, Dannion Brinkley. Villard Books, New York, 1994

*Transformed By The Light: The Powerful Effect of Near-Death
Experiences on People's Lives,* Melvin Morse, M.D. Ballantine Books,
New York, 1992.

Out-of Body Experiences

Far Journeys, Robert A. Monroe. Doubleday, New York, 1987.

Journeys Our of the Body, Robert A. Monroe. Doubleday, New York,
1977.

Paradox

Paradoxes For Living: Cultivating Faith in Confusing Times, N. Graham
Standish. Westminster John Knox Press, Louisville, KY, 2001.

Past Lives

Journey of Souls: Case Studies of Life Between Lives, Michael Newton,
Ph.D. Lewellyn Publications, St. Paul, MN, 1994.

*Returning From the Light: Using Past Lives to Understand the Present
and Shape the Future,* Brad Steiger. Signet, New York, 1996.

Reincarnation

Lifecycles: Reincarnation and the Web of Life, Christopher M. Bache,
Ph.D. Paragon House, New York, 1994.

Many Lives, Many Masters, Brian L. Weiss, M.D. Simon and Shuster,
New York, 1988.

Other Lives, Other Selves, Roger J. Woolger, Ph.D. Doubleday, New
York, 1987.

SUGGESTED READING LIST

Reincarnation: An East-West Anthology, Joseph Head and S. L. Cranston. Theosophical Publishing House, Wheaton, IL, 1961.

Reincarnation: The Missing Link in Christianity, Elizabeth Clare Prophet. Summit University Press, Corwin Springs, MT, 1997.

Reincarnation: The Phoenix Fire Mystery, Joseph Head and S. L. Cranston. Warner Books, New York, 1979.

Spirituality

Celestine Prophecy, The: An Adventure, James Redfield. Warner Books, New York, 1993.

Conversations with God: An Uncommon Dialogue, Books 1, 2 and 3, Neale Donald Walsch. G. P. Putnam's Sons, New York, 1996-1998.

Eagle and the Rose, The, Rosemary Altea. Warner Books, New York, 1995.

Proud Spirit: Lessons, Insights and Healing from "The Voice of the Spirit World", Rosemary Altea. William Morrow, NY, 1997.

Rolling Thunder: An exploration into the secret healing powers of an American Indian medicine man, Doug Boyd. Bantam Doubleday, New York, 1974.

Seat of the Soul, The, Gary Zukav. Simon and Schuster, NY, 1989.

Soul Stories, Gary Zukav. Simon and Schuster, New York, 2000.

The Coming of the Cosmic Christ, Matthew Fox. Harper and Row, San Francisco, 1988.

You Own The Power: Stories and Exercises to Inspire and Unleash the Force Within, Rosemary Altea. William Morrow, NY, 2000.

Visionary Experiences

Coming From the Light: Spiritual Accounts of Life Before Life, Sarah Hinze. Simon and Schuster, New York, 1994.

I Am With You Always: True Stories of Encounters with Jesus, G. Scott Sparrow, Ed.D. Bantam Books, New York, 1995.

Parting Visions: Uses and Meanings of Pre-Death, Psychic, and Spiritual Experiences, Melvin Morse, M.D. Harper, New York, 1994.

Notes

---

1 John 16:12, TEV
2 Matt. 28:20, RSV
3 John 14:12
4 John 11:47-50
5 John 16:13
6 Matt. 16:24, TEV, italics added
7 John 16:12
8 I Cor. 9:22, TEV
9 John 14:2-4, Matt. 28:7
10 Princeton Seminary Bulletin, XXII-1, 2001, p. 8.
11 John 16:12-13
12 Matt. 28:20, TEV
13 Matt. 18:20, RSV
14 James 1:13
15 Mark 15:34, TEV
16 John 14:12, TEV
17 Fynn. William Collins Sons, London, 1974, p. 143.
18 Nov. 24, 2000
19 Matt. 26:41, RSV
20 John 4:24, TEV
21 *Readers' Digest,* March, 2000, p. 175.
22 Gen. 1:26, RSV
23 John 10:30, TEV
24 *Anna's Book*, Fynn. Ballantine, 1986, p. 38.
25 Psalm 46:10, RSV
26 John 14:6, RSV. This statement is dealt with in Chapter 13.
27 Mark 9:23, TEV
28 Mark 11:24, TEV
29 *New Castle News,* New Castle, PA, 1-31-01.
30 Matt. 18:6, TEV
31 Mark 12:38-40, TEV, adapted
32 Matt. 7:21, TEV
33 Psalm 46:10, RSV
34 Heb. 5:13-14, TEV
35 *The Messengers*, *The True Story of Angelic Presence and the Return to the Age of Miracles*, by Julia Ingram and G.W. Hardin. This 1996 book talks about Nick Bunick who received an angel message one day at 4:44 a.m. He began to notice this number frequently thereafter, and came to understand that it is a symbol for the power of God's love. Thousands of people have had "444" experiences, and there are a number of websites which contain their stories.

[36] *Galileo's Daughter* by Dava Sobel. Walker and Company, New York, 1999, page 249.

[37] Bernie Siegel

[38] Encyclopedia Britannica.

[39] Eph. 1:4, TEV

[40] Matt. 16:14, TEV

[41] "God is Great!"

[42] Josh. 11:6 - God promises to kill Israel's enemies at Merom Brook; plus numerous other examples.

[43] Ex. 21:7, rules about selling a daughter into slavery.

[44] Deut. 21:20-21, stoning to death a rebellious son; Ex. 21:15, 17, killing a child who hits or curses his parents.

[45] Solomon had 700 wives - I Kings 11:3; also Ex. 21:10

[46] Ex. 21:20-21 where a slave is considered property; also Titus 2:9 where slaves are told to submit to their masters.

[47] I Cor. 14:34-35, Women are not allowed to speak in church.

[48] I Cor. 6:9, "homosexual perverts."

[49] Gen. 3:16

[50] John 1:5, TEV

[51] Matt. 7:21-23, TEV

[52] Matt. 16:24

[53] Matt. 5:9

[54] Gal. 6:7

[55] Luke 6:31, TEV

[56] Mt. 5:46,48, TEV

[57] Swami Shivananda, one of Ramakrishna's disciples.

[58] p. 194

[59] John 10:30, TEV

[60] John 14:12, TEV

[61] John 10:34, TEV

[62] John 8:12

[63] Matt. 5:14, RSV

[64] John 14:6, TEV

[65] Delta, 1995, pp. 95-96.

[66] Mark 1:15

[67] John 5:1-9

[68] John 3:3, TEV

[69] Phil. 2:12

[70] Horticulture (the sower, the weeds, the mustard seed); baking (the yeast); real estate (the hidden treasure); investments (the pearl); fishing (the net): Matt. 13:18-50.

[71] Matt. 13:35, TEV

[72] Luke 24:13-35

NOTES

[73] Luke 24:39

[74] John 14:19, RSV

[75] http://www.angelscribe.com/1111stor.html.

[76] Matt. 7:2, RSV